# Relative Truth, Ultimate Truth

THE FOUNDATION OF BUDDHIST THOUGHT SERIES

# Relative Truth, Ultimate Truth

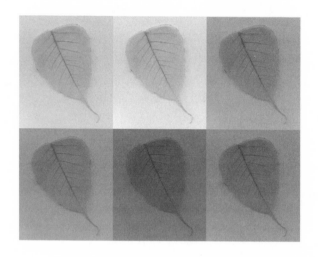

## THE FOUNDATION of BUDDHIST THOUGHT

VOLUME 2

# GESHE TASHI TSERING

FOREWORD BY LAMA ZOPA RINPOCHE

EDITED BY GORDON MCDOUGALL

WISDOM PUBLICATIONS ✦ BOSTON

Wisdom Publications, Inc.
199 Elm Street
Somerville MA 02144 USA
www.wisdompubs.org

*Library of Congress Cataloging-in-Publication Data*
Tashi Tsering, Geshe, 1958–
Relative truth, ultimate truth / Geshe Tashi Tsering ; foreword by Lama Zopa Rinpoche ; edited by Gordon McDougall.
  p. cm. — (The foundation of Buddhist thought ; v. 2)
ISBN 0-86171-271-4 (pbk. : alk. paper)
1. Truth—Religious aspects—Buddhism. 2. Buddhism—Doctrines. I. McDougall, Gordon, 1948– II. Title.
BQ4255.T38 2008
294.3'420423—dc22

                              2008022857


ISBN 0-86171-271-4
12 11 10 09 08
5  4  3  2  1

Cover and interior design by Gopa&Ted2, Inc. Set in Goudy 10.5/16 pt.

Wisdom Publications' books are printed on acid-free paper and meet the guidelines for permanence and durability set by the Committee on Production Guidelines for Book Longevity of the Council on Library Resources.

Printed in the United States of America

This book was produced with environmental mindfulness. We have elected to print this title on 30% PCW recycled paper. As a result, we have saved the following resources: 12 trees, 8 million BTUs of energy, 1,056 lbs. of greenhouse gases, 4,385 gallons of water, and 563 lbs. of solid waste. For more information, please visit our website, www.wisdompubs.org. This paper is also FSC certified. For more information, please visit www.fscus.org.

# CONTENTS

# Foreword

THE BUDDHA'S MESSAGE is universal. We all search for happiness but somehow fail to find it because we are looking for it in the wrong way. Only when we start cherishing others will true happiness grow within us, and so the Buddha's essential teaching is one of compassion and ethics, combined with the wisdom that understands the nature of reality. The teachings of the Buddha contain everything needed to eliminate suffering and make life truly meaningful, and as such the teachings are not only relevant in today's world but vital.

This is the message that my precious teacher, Lama Thubten Yeshe, gave to his Western students. His vision to present the Dharma in a way that is accessible and relevant to everyone continues and grows. His organization, the Foundation for the Preservation of the Mahayana Tradition (FPMT), now has centers all over the world, and Lama's work is carried on by many of his students.

*The Foundation of Buddhist Thought*, developed by Geshe Tashi Tsering, is one of the core courses of the FPMT's integrated education program. The essence of Tibetan Buddhist philosophy can be found within its six subjects. *The Foundation of Buddhist Thought* serves as a wonderful basis for further study in Buddhism, as well as a tool to transform our everyday lives.

Geshe Tashi has been the resident teacher at Jamyang Buddhist

Centre, London, since 1994. He has been very beneficial in guiding the students there and in many other centers where he teaches. Besides his profound knowledge—he is a Lharampa geshe, the highest educational qualification within our tradition—his excellent English and his deep understanding of his Western students means that he can present the Dharma in a way that is both accessible and relevant. His wisdom, compassion, and humor are combined with a genuine gift as a teacher. You will see within the six books of the *Foundation of Buddhist Thought* series the same combination of profound understanding and heart advice that can guide beginners and experienced Dharma practitioners alike on the spiritual path.

Whether you read this book out of curiosity or as a part of your spiritual journey, I sincerely hope that you find it beneficial and that it shows you a way to open your heart and develop your wisdom.

Lama Zopa Rinpoche
Spiritual Director
Foundation for the Preservation of the Mahayana Tradition

# PREFACE

THE SUBJECT OF THE SECOND of the *Foundation of Buddhist Thought* series is the two truths of relative and ultimate truth. This is a subject I encountered when I was a young monk in the monastery and as an enthusiastic debater I was immediately fascinated by it. It soon became clear to me, however, that this was much more than just something philosophical, something to challenge a young mind; this was something incredibly relevant to my daily life. To see how there is a mismatch between the reality of how things exist and how we perceive they exist, and to see how these two levels of conventional and ultimate reality are intertwined in every thing we do, can bring a richness to our lives and has the potential to really help us out of our problems. Once I saw this, I was hooked.

From that time on I have been amazed at how many different ways these two truths operate in our lives. It is not as if one is a purely theoretical debating point or the other is pure fantasy; both function on their particular level. On the conventional level, my life, like all our lives, has its share of joy, fulfillment, pain, and challenges, all tied together through the ever-evolving chains of cause and effect that dominate what I do and who I am. All this is real. It is real because I experience it and because I see it operating within the lives of everyone I encounter: my friends, my family, my colleagues. On a relative

level, I need to work on what skills I have to make the best of the cir-
cumstances I meet everyday in order to have as peaceful and calm a
life as possible.

But to really be effective at this I need to understand what is happening at a deeper level. Beyond the conventional causal dependen-
cies that rule our lives, there is a fundamental mode of existence that
all things and events share; that is ultimate truth. At this level all
things melt into the same taste beyond diversity. I find it utterly fascinating that beyond the myriad things that make up our universe
there lies this deeper level of reality, one where there is no diversity,
no difference. To come to even a very superficial understanding of
this is, I think, a huge help in seeing how and why things happen in
the way they do, and so start to be able to overcome the difficulties
we now face.

And so I think the two truths are a vital part of the spiritual journey we must all undertake if we want to rise above the confusion
and pain of this world. Based on these two levels of reality the
entire Buddhist practice is developed. It is extremely clear, for
example, that we need an understanding of the two truths if we
want to really understand the Buddha's first teaching, the four
noble truths, and if we want to take the first serious step as a Buddhist by taking refuge. As His Holiness the Dalai Lama said in *The
Four Noble Truths*:

> Only when you have an understanding of the nature and rela-
> tionship of these Two Truths are you in a position to fully
> understand the meaning of the Four Noble Truths. And once
> you understand the Four Noble Truths, then you have a sound
> foundation on which to develop a good understanding of what
> is meant by Taking Refuge in the Three Jewels.[1]

He is echoing the words of so many of the great teachers that have gone before him, like the great Indian masters Nagarjuna and Chandrakirti. Actually the two truths is not just a vital subject within Buddhism, but also in the non-Buddhist philosophical traditions. So many philosophies try to explain the disparity between how things exist and how we ordinary people perceive them to exist, and emphasize how vital this understanding is in solving our problems.

When I first prepared *The Foundation of Buddhist Thought* as a series I seriously contemplated making the two truths the first topic to be covered, as this is the right and proper sequence of any spiritual path. I was very concerned however that as an introduction to Buddhism it might seem too abstract and dry, and so I have made this the second book. Far from being abstract and dry, though, I find this subject is so rich, and I hope you will come to share my enthusiasm for it.

The two truths is probably my favorite subject but that doesn't mean that I understand it, especially as presented by the highest school, Prasangika. There is still a long way to go, and even these days I ask questions, by phone or on a cassette, of my own wonderful teacher, Geshe Thubten Renchen, who has taught me since my first days in the monastery and is still immensely kind and helpful. And many other great teachers like His Holiness the Dalai Lama have helped me to understand this topic in many different ways. For all of them I have great admiration and a deep feeling of closeness. There is no way I could repay their kindness, even over many lifetimes, but I would like to take this opportunity, with deep respect and hands folded at my heart, to thank all these great teachers, who have helped me understand the amazing teachings like the two truths.

With my lack of understanding, I'm sure there are many mistakes, and this book is quite elementary compared with the other profound works on the subject, but I sincerely hope it will help you in some way. As such, I would like to encourage you to share my enthusiasm for the two truths and to read it with as open a mind as possible.

# Editor's Preface

I HAD BEEN LISTENING to teachings on Buddhism for about ten years when in the introduction to a teaching on emptiness I first heard the term *the two truths*. It was described as probably the most important concept in Buddhism. If that were so, I wondered, why was there so little material about it available in English?

Very soon afterward, in 1997, Geshe Tashi started the *Foundation of Buddhist Thought* study program, the second module of which was about the two truths, and at the end of the four months I thought I knew why. I was happy to relegate the two truths to the "esoteric and interesting but not for me" drawer. It has only been thanks to repeated exposure to this subject that I have slowly come to realize how crucial it is for us to understand how we misread reality and how we can perceive reality correctly (the heart of the two truths) if we really want to get to the bottom of why we suffer.

One of the things that has delighted me both as a student of *The Foundation of Buddhist Thought* and as its former administrator has been the way the parts of the course fit so neatly into the whole. The first three subjects—the four noble truths, the two truths, and Buddhist psychology—are the groundwork, the knowledge we need to really progress spiritually, and the other three subjects—bodhichitta, emptiness, and tantra—are the actual practice. Put together they make a glorious whole, and areas of one subject dovetail into and crop up again in other subjects, serving to clarify and consolidate. One student of the course summed it up by saying that "the jigsaw puzzle that is the Dharma now all fits into place."

There is no more crucial piece of the jigsaw puzzle than the two truths. We are trying to develop both our emotional, compassionate side and our intelligent, logical side, the "method" and "wisdom" Buddhism so often refers to, which are like two wings of a bird, both of which are needed to fly. On one level we are increasing our positive potential and eliminating our negative qualities. This requires the conventional mind to deal with relative truths. We are also trying to gain the wisdom that will overcome the root of our suffering, which requires the mind to explore the ultimate nature of things and events. Before getting too far, then, it stands to reason that we must be clear about these two modes of existence—not just the disparity between them but also their similarity.

This is why I feel we have such a gem with Geshe Tashi, who not only has a profound knowledge of the subject from his study at Sera Monastery but also the ability to render it in clear and accessible English, from his many years living and working in an English-speaking environment and his intense study of how Westerners think. Moreover, as I am sure you will have already learned if you have read any of the other *Foundation of Buddhist Thought* books or have had the opportunity to listen to Geshe Tashi teach, he has a natural flair for delivering the Dharma in a way that is lively, inspiring, and very relevant.

Even so, getting this book ready for publication has been hard work. From the original course book, which was a reworking of transcripts of the first two *Foundation of Buddhist Thought* London courses, Geshe-la then taught much of the two truths again in an attempt to clarify for himself how to tackle the areas within the subject. This was reworked into the first draft, which he almost summarily abandoned. And from a second draft, there has been more major reworking. I think I can safely say that any lack of clarity comes from the inadequacies of the editor, not the writer.

I first met Geshe Tashi in 1992, when he was staying at Nalanda Monastery in southern France, studying both the English language and the Western mind. I thought him remarkable then, but only started to see the natural teacher in him when he moved to Jamyang Buddhist Centre in London soon after that.

Born in Purang, Tibet, in 1958, Geshe Tashi escaped to India with his parents one year later. He entered Sera Mey Monastic University at thirteen, and spent the next sixteen years working for his geshe degree, graduating as a Lharampa geshe, the highest possible degree.

After a year at the Highest Tantric College (Gyuto), Geshe-la began his teaching career in Kopan Monastery near Kathmandu, the principal monastery of the Foundation for the Preservation of the Mahayana Tradition (FPMT). Geshe Tashi then moved to the Gandhi Foundation College in Nagpur, and it was at that time that the FPMT's Spiritual Director, Lama Thubten Zopa Rinpoche, asked him to teach in the West. After two years at Nalanda Monastery in France, Geshe Tashi became the resident teacher at Jamyang Buddhist Centre in London in 1994.

Very early on in his teaching career at Jamyang, he observed that the passive, text-based learning usually associated with Tibetan Buddhist teachings in Western Dharma centers often failed to engage the students in a meaningful way. In an effort to provide an alternative to this traditional teaching approach while giving his students a solid overview of Buddhism, he devised a two-year, six-module study program that incorporated Western pedagogic methods. As I have said, this book has grown out of the second course book of this study program, *The Foundation of Buddhist Thought*.

As with the other books in the series, many people have been involved with the development of this volume and I would like to thank them all. I would also like to offer my warmest thanks to Lama Zopa Rinpoche, the head of the FPMT and the inspiration for the group of study programs to which *The Foundation of Buddhist Thought* belongs.

# 1 THE EVOLUTION OF BUDDHIST THOUGHT

## Logic and Emotion

### THE LONG VIEW

IN THE VAST TEACHINGS given by the Buddha in the more than forty years between his enlightenment and his parinirvana, he addressed the fundamental philosophical questions of what is reality and how can we know it extensively and often. Behaving ethically and mastering the mind through meditation are important aspects of our lives, but so too is understanding the nature of reality. Quite simply, we suffer because we misconceive reality.

The main focus of Buddhist philosophy has always been the nature of reality. For over 2,500 years since the Buddha's time, scholars have been studying his words in order to understand exactly what this reality is. In Buddhist philosophy, when we speak of how things exist and how we perceive they exist, we are talking about the two truths: ultimate truth and conventional, or relative, truth.

Coming to terms with the essence of Buddhist thought is not easy. There are many alien concepts and many very subtle ideas that will not make sense immediately or without effort. If we can see how vital this understanding is and apply ourselves diligently, things will become clearer as time passes. A long view is needed, and both the emotional and the logical sides of our nature need to be nurtured together. Only by developing a good heart will we truly become a better person, and only by seeing the reality of our situation will we be able to improve it in a truly meaningful way.

Why do we make mistakes? We need to explore this vital question to see that we suffer because we fail to see how things exist. Ourselves, other people, objects such as our possessions, the events in our lives—the things of which our world is comprised—are constantly misunderstood on a very subtle level, and it is this gap between reality and how we conceive reality that leads to not just some of our problems but *all* of our problems. That gap is called *ignorance*.

Our universe is made up of things and events. Some of these may be pure fantasies or simply not exist, but the vast majority exist and function, and at one level we are unmistaken in how we perceive them. That is conventional truth. At a more subtle level however, we fail to see the way they come into existence due to causes and conditions and the way we erroneously ascribe to them a concrete reality. The mode of existence of phenomena at this deeper "ultimate" level is ultimate truth. Narrowing the gap between how things appear to exist and how they actually exist is the focus of this book.

Based on misinformation, we make judgments, mistakes arise, and we suffer. The more accurate our vision of reality is, the more informed our judgments will be, and therefore fewer mistakes and less suffering will occur. Our habitual misreading of reality is so deep-rooted, however, that it is not simply a matter of studying it once and being cured. It takes time to make a true connection with the essence of Buddhist philosophy and to inculcate it within our daily lives on a sufficiently deep level that we can break our present harmful habits.

This is not abstract philosophy, nor is it an interesting but irrelevant mind game. This is the vital key to real happiness. As long as we are perpetually tied up in misconceptions about the nature of reality—

in particular, as long as we see our own sense of identity as static and eternal—we will forever reify objects and situations, and due to this, we will continue to develop attachment and aversion. Locked into a worldview where "I" is the center and all else must serve the "I," we have no space to help others and, paradoxically, no space to be happy.

The more egocentric we are, the tighter our mind is, and consequently the unhappier we are. Only by seeing how we misconceive both the "I" and the universe that this "I" inhabits will we be able to break away from the rigid me-me-me space we inhabit now and loosen up into a lighter, happier mindset that cherishes others. This is the goal.

## Harnessing Our Emotions

The purpose of Buddhist philosophy is to bring us to an accurate understanding of how the world exists in order to develop our minds to be of most benefit. We need to marry this logical side with our natural emotional side. Emotion alone will not take us very far. Compassion is vital, otherwise the selfish mind will lead us to harm others and, paradoxically, ourselves. However, if that compassion is not supported by the right view of reality, then it will be flawed. We have all seen people who are full of compassion but very short on wisdom and who, despite their good intentions, seem to harm more than help. We need love, compassion, altruism, and all the positive aspects of our emotional life, but we need wisdom as well. Right view and compassion conjoined give us an unbeatable tool to develop our full potential— the potential to free ourselves from both short-term and long-term suffering and to effectively help others out of their suffering.

The quest for the truth leads us through unfamiliar philosophies and alien cultures, and it takes a degree of faith that the early Buddhist philosophers were on the right track in their search. By "faith"

I don't mean a blind faith in religious dogma. Instead, I'm talking about a deeply felt conviction that because the ideas of Buddhism work on all the levels we do understand, those we cannot yet understand are, therefore, probably equally valid—it is just that we have not reached that level of understanding yet. As the wonderful Indian poet and philosopher Rabindranath Tagore wrote:

> Faith is a bird that feels the light
> and sings when the dawn is still dark.[2]

I'm not saying that non-Buddhists blindly accept whereas Buddhists understand. Far from it! People of every religion and philosophy tend to hear the tenets of their own religion and simply accept them, rather than do the hard work of understanding them.

We need every tool at our disposal to shed light on the reality of our lives and break us free from the sloth of our mundane thinking. We have leisure, intelligence, an inquisitive nature that our culture does not suppress, and we have met teachings such as this. I think that when we are struggling with these very esoteric topics, there is a tendency to be overwhelmed. However, by carefully examining their importance and the rarity and preciousness of this opportunity we now have, we will be able to break through the fog of misunderstanding and start to see a glimmer of the meaning of the two truths.

Understanding emptiness (a synonym for ultimate truth) is difficult. Even His Holiness the Dalai Lama has said that his study of emptiness has been a major aspect of his philosophical study since he was sixteen, but only now can he see some light at the end of the tunnel. Fortunately, we don't need a full understanding of emptiness in order to benefit. In his *Four Hundred Stanzas* (*Chatuhshataka*), Aryadeva says:

Even those with few merits
Have no doubts about this Dharma [emptiness].
Even those who still have their doubts
Will tear [cyclic] existence to tatters.[3]

Just starting to doubt whether things and events exist inherently really goes a long way toward understanding reality. In this world of billions of people (and countless other sentient beings), very few really try to understand whether appearance matches reality. This doubt about the intrinsic nature of things is an exceptional quality. It actually approaches a real understanding of emptiness and, thus, of ultimate truth. To come to know how the world truly exists, we first need to know how it *appears* to exist for us; thus, it is vital to understand relative, or conventional, truth as well. In fact, one cannot become a fully realized being without understanding both conventional truth and ultimate truth.

We have freedom and intelligence and we know that through our study of the two truths there is the possibility that we can truly free ourselves from samsara. So really, we have no choice; we have to try, no matter how hard it is. Even having the smallest doubt that the world is exactly as we perceive it "tears cyclic existence to tatters." That's quite a challenge!

From my own side, I can see how routine and ordinary the vast majority of my thoughts and actions are. I wake up and simply follow the flow of my ordinary thoughts wherever they take me. Whether my thoughts move in a positive or a negative direction, my mind simply follows, like debris drifting on a river's current. Generally, my mind is quite neutral and not very active. Of course, I act—I walk, eat, talk, read, and so forth—but I wouldn't call that active. That is simply the mind and body trudging along the well-worn tracks of utterly routine and, for the most part, boring habits.

For a purposeful and fruitful life, therefore, we need a long vision that allows us to marry logic and emotion in ways that are meaningful. We need to address the fundamental questions that plague all of us. At the end of the day, the philosophy we accept must impact our everyday activities or it will end up a mere abstraction, utterly worthless.

But where exactly do the two truths fit in to our lives? How can they be more than a religious idea, a piece of dogma we are given to absorb somehow, perhaps by placing it on an altar and bowing before it? When we see a bar of chocolate, for instance, we generally feel no need to philosophize about it. (Of course, if we're on a diet, that is another thing!) What do the two truths have to do with that?

Could studying itself be therapeutic, regardless of the truth of Buddhism's claims? Perhaps we gain some psychological advantage just by investigating the question of what is real. If the two truths really do describe how things are, how does exploring that relationship become anything more than an intellectual exercise? How does it change our very perception and experience of the world? The process of finding the answer to this question is the process of enlightenment itself. It's up to you how you approach it—religiously, philosophically, or therapeutically. To be successful, you will likely need to draw on each of these approaches at some point or other.

The Buddha showed us that the peace we all seek is not to be found in the extremes—neither in the reification of things and events nor in nihilistically denying they exist—but in the middle way. The middle ground between seeing things as utterly solid or as completely unreal is a very subtle place.

## Listening, Contemplating, and Meditating

Initially it is very important for us to read, listen, and discuss the various topics we are studying. Without having enough information there is nothing to contemplate, and if there is nothing to contemplate, then there is nothing to meditate on. To use the rather cruel traditional analogy, it is like a fingerless person trying to climb a mountain of ice—nothing to hold on to and no means of holding.

This first aspect of understanding, *listening*, is the initial step of our spiritual development, no matter what form it takes: listening, reading, discussing, or even watching His Holiness the Dalai Lama on a DVD.

As we embark on this voyage into the nature of reality, we need many different skills. We need to be selective in our reading and listening, sifting out the authentic texts from those that can lead us astray, so an element of discrimination is needed. The authentic texts, such as the sutras themselves and their commentaries, are often dense and couched in unfamiliar terms; we need a good deal of intelligence to tackle them. We also need perseverance, since to get at their actual meaning we will have to study them and listen to teachings on them from qualified masters again and again.

A Tibetan master has said that if the food is delicious and you don't have any teeth, then you need to chew with your gums. We are presently toothless. (As well as fingerless—we're in a bad way!) Just because it is hard to understand the great texts does not mean we should find more easily digestible but less tasty ones. Many Buddhist philosophical works were written for Tibetan monastics and in an archaic style; consequently, they can be quite dense. Yet if you read them again and again—chewing with your gums—they will get richer and richer. It's amazing how a good novel can keep you absorbed for hours, but a Dharma book can send you to sleep after only a page. Nevertheless, by persevering, understanding will come.

Listening without assimilating what we are listening to is useless, of course, so the second step is *contemplating*, which means absorbing more deeply whatever we have heard, into our hearts. For instance, hearing that ignorance is the root of samsara will not get us any closer to freedom from suffering unless we apply that knowledge. So we need to contemplate the meaning, explore whether it is true, and then apply it to our lives.

Contemplation means to investigate what we have heard, to come to know as much as we can about it, and to understand it as deeply as we can. Only then are we ready to start *meditating* on it, which is the third of the three steps to understanding. You can see that meditation comes quite late in the process. This is not to say that you shouldn't be earnestly trying to develop your vital meditation skills now. But without a fairly profound understanding of the subject, there is little to meditate on apart from closing our eyes and peacefully staying still. To get to the level of understanding where meditating on a topic becomes truly fruitful, we need to have already contemplated it, and fruitful contemplation requires prior listening. There is no way to skip a step. We truly need a long view.

## The Evolution of Buddhist Thought

If you were to ask me, as a Tibetan monk from the monastic system, what the final view of Buddhist thought is, I would say that it is the Prasangika Madhyamaka view that all things and events are free of any intrinsic reality. That does not mean, however, that we should only study the Prasangika Madhyamaka system. A clear understanding of the evolution of the philosophical systems allows us to see and appreciate the ever-growing subtlety of the view. In actuality, it is very difficult to jump to the final view without a grounding in the "lower" or less subtle systems, in the same way as it would be foolhardy to attempt a Ph.D. before completing one's bachelor's or master's degrees.

Historically and logically it appears that one school grew from another and that different views emerged gradually and were "created" by different scholars; but we need to be very clear that there is nothing here that the Buddha did not teach. All the shades of philosophy studied in the Tibetan monasteries come from the Buddha. He taught not only the Pali sutras that are studied in the Theravada schools, but also the Perfection of Wisdom (*prajñaparamita*) sutras from the so-called second turning of the Dharma wheel and the *Buddha Nature Sutra* (*Tathagatagarbha Sutra*) from the third turning.

What follows in this volume is my understanding of what I was taught. Current historical evidence does not support such clear boundaries between the various Buddhist schools in India, but in the monastic education I received, historical accuracy was not the main point when studying philosophical views. What mattered was the depth of our understanding. Studying the views of the lower schools made our grasp of the highest view that much more subtle and precise.

## BUDDHISM IN INDIA

Buddhism in India can roughly be divided into three stages. Without written records of the first stage—the time of the Buddha and soon after—there is a lot of confusion about dates and concepts. It is further confused by the fact that, like most religions, Buddhism did not arise fully grown from an empty arena but developed within a richly cultured and philosophical society with already well-established religions, such as Brahmanism and Jainism. For a long period there was no such term as "Buddhism," and the Buddha's followers were thought of no differently than the followers of many of the other masters around at that time.

The Buddha's students were neither many nor influential, and because many of the subjects that the Buddha taught, such as the law of cause and effect (*karma*) and liberation (*moksha*), already existed within the other traditions, it is not necessarily true that the Buddha attracted followers because of new radical teachings. Only slowly did Buddhist views become distinguishable from other existing views and become a separate philosophy, and this was often as a reaction to the demands or constraints of society.

The first survival stage lasted about two hundred years until the time of King Ashoka, whose reign marked the start of Buddhism's second stage in India. Ashoka ruled almost the whole of India and had converted to Buddhism; consequently, during his reign Buddhism became a strong and separate religion, rather than being mixed up in the public's mind with Brahmanism or Jainism, as it had been previously. By 250 B.C.E. the Buddha's teachings were quite established and respected; hence, his followers had more opportunity to debate on the exact meaning of what the Buddha had taught.

The Buddha's teachings are usually divided into three baskets or *pitakas*: the Vinaya Pitaka, the Abhidharma Pitaka, and the Sutra Pitaka. The Vinaya basket discourses are mainly concerned with the rules and regulations of the monastic community, whereas the Sutra basket comprises the bulk of the teachings of the Buddha, those on developing compassion, concentration, and so on. There was never much debate about these two baskets, but the Abhidharma teachings, which deal with philosophy, were debated extensively. It is often the case that once a philosophy becomes established, then there is time to reflect on the meaning of the teaching in all its detail. So it was with Buddhism. The debates really started once Buddhism became strong and established in India. This in turn led to sectarian development, with some practitioners leaning toward one developing system of ideas and other practitioners toward another.

These rigorous debates took place in many universities, the greatest of which was Nalanda, located north of Bodhgaya in India. From

about 200 C.E. to about 1200 C.E. tens of thousands of scholars studied and debated with an incredible intensity and single-mindedness.

With the growing need to clarify concepts and to defend Buddhist ideas from the criticisms of non-Buddhist scholars, Buddhist
practitioners worked hard at establishing exactly what Buddhism
defined as truth, which inevitably led to disagreements and differing
opinions.

In India, the Abhidharma texts were the main debating point
because they explained the nature of reality of things and events. The
Buddha's teachings clearly denied the existence of an ultimate creator, so using the doctrine of cause and effect, these early works sought
to find logical explanations for how and why things come into existence. In ways that would seem very familiar to modern scientists,
they relentlessly divided and subdivided the objects of the known
world in an attempt to reach the basic building block of the universe.
Belief in the reality of atom-like building blocks is a hallmark of the
Vaibhashika, or Great Exposition, school.

Then more radical views emerged, calling into question whether
such a basic universal building block existed from its own side (a bit
like the way quantum physicists radicalized the world of physics). This
far-from-traditional interpretation of the Abhidharma texts started
around the time of Nagarjuna and his student Aryadeva. It is generally agreed that Nagarjuna lived in the second century C.E. and was
the founder of the Madhyamaka, or Middle Way, school.

The third stage of Buddhism in India began with a surge of development in more sophisticated philosophical tools. Logical reasoning
reached a new level with Dignaga (ca. 450) and his follower Dharmakirti (ca. 625). They refined the use of logic and contributed new
and sophisticated epistemological tools to the larger philosophical
discussion of the time. In addition, the texts explaining their system
of thought brought a completely new understanding about the mind

and standardized the presentation of Buddhist psychology. These presentations form the basis for the Sautrantika, or Sutra, school of Buddhism.

Buddhapalita and his contemporary Bhavaviveka (sixth century) both claimed to be Madhyamikas and followers of Nagarjuna, but Bhavaviveka strongly attacked Buddhapalita's commentary on Nagarjuna's *Fundamental Treatise on the Middle Way* (*Mulamadhyamaka*) and defeated Buddhapalita's followers in debate. Later, Chandrakirti (seventh century) resuscitated Buddhapalita's views and attacked the position of Bhavaviveka. Chandrakirti's works eventually became central to the Tibetan interpretation of Madhyamaka philosophy, especially within the Gelug school, and for this reason Bhavaviveka is often depicted in a negative light by Gelug commentators. The split between Bhavaviveka's views and those of Chandrakirti form the basis for dividing Madhyamikas into *Svatantrika* (autonomy) and *Prasangika* (consequence).

Next, we find two brothers, Asanga and Vasubandhu (fourth century). The elder, Asanga, created a system of philosophy that became the Chittamatra (Mind Only) school, also called the Yogachara school, which asserts that external objects have no reality separate from the consciousness that perceives them. This, he claimed was the middle way between the realism of Vaibhashika and the nihilism of Madhyamaka. (Madhyamaka scholars, not surprisingly, see themselves as holding the middle way, and Chittamatra concepts as idealism.) Asanga and Vasubandhu also wrote the Abhidharma texts that are most authoritative for Tibetan Buddhism.

## THE FOUR SCHOOLS

This gives you some sense of the historical basis for what the Tibetan tradition identifies as the four Buddhist schools. These are:

+ Vaibhashika
+ Sautrantika
+ Chittamatra
+ Madhyamaka

The first two schools, the *Vaibhashika* (Great Exposition) school and the *Sautrantika* (Sutra) school, searched for the basic building block of the universe, and because these basic particles were seen as truly existent, these two schools are known as *realist* schools. These two schools assert only the selflessness of persons, not the selflessness of phenomena.

With the third school, the *Chittamatra* (Mind Only) school, the intrinsic reality of external objects is questioned. It is argued that whereas the mind is real, the objects perceived by the mind cannot have independent existence because of that very reliance on the mind to ascertain them.

Finally, there is the *Madhyamaka* (Middle Way) school, the fourth and (so my tradition considers) "highest," or most subtle school. The Madhyamaka view is the "middle way" because its position lies between what it sees as the *eternalism* of the first two schools that sees objects as existing from their own side, and the *nihilism* of the Chittamatra school that asserts that things and events have no reality at all.

The four schools are divided into the non-Mahayana schools of Vaibhashika and Sautrantika and the Mahayana schools of Chittamatra and Madhyamaka. In addition to their assertion that things exist independently, the first two schools' view of karma and cyclic existence is simpler than that of the later schools and can be of more immediate impact in our daily lives. The Mahayana schools would argue, however, that their philosophies cannot take us all the way to enlightenment. In very general terms, the first two schools work toward achieving individual liberation whereas the Mahayana tradition works toward attaining full enlightenment in order to free all beings from suffering.

All the philosophical schools have subdivisions—none are as neat as the texts suggest—but the most important subdivision for us is the division of the Madhyamaka school into the Svatantrika Madhyamaka and the Prasangika Madhyamaka subschools. Such a distinction was not made in India. When Buddhist philosophy was studied in Tibet, however, these different views were regarded as quite separate; in Tibetan writings they appear almost as two completely different schools. In this way, the Svatantrika became another "lower" school to be refuted.

## BUDDHISM IN TIBET

Before Buddhism, Tibet had its own native shamanistic religion called Bön. It was natural that as Buddhism gradually became established, Bön ideas and practices merged with the new religion to influence what was to become Tibetan Buddhism. There are still Bön practitioners in Tibetan communities today.

The influx of Buddhism into Tibet happened over two main periods, called the two disseminations. Although at the time Buddhism was already being practiced by some individual practitioners, the first dissemination is said to have dated from around 617 C.E., when Songtsen Gampo, the Tibetan king who was to become very important to Buddhism, sent people trained in Sanskrit to India to study Buddhism.

The next king of Tibet, Trisong Detsen, worked with Padmasambhava and Shantarakshita to make Buddhism the state religion. Padmasambhava founded the first tradition of Tibetan Buddhism, the Nyingma, and developed the ritual side of Buddhism to fit in with the then-existing very ritualistic system of Bön. He and Shantarakshita

also founded the first monastery, Samye, and Shantarakshita intro-
duced Madhyamaka philosophy to Tibet, specifically the views of the
Svatantrika Madhyamaka subschool.

The next king, Langdarma, was very opposed to Buddhism and
almost destroyed it, forcing it underground for almost a hundred years.
During that time, Buddhist practitioners were only able to practice
clandestinely in caves. Although Langdarma only reigned for four or
five years, the repercussions were enormous and severe. Books and
monasteries were destroyed, and it took a long time for Buddhism to
be reestablished there.

The second dissemination started in the eleventh century with
Lotsawa Rinchen Sangpo (lotsawa means "translator"), who translated a great many of the texts that had been destroyed. By then
Nalanda was starting to crumble under the waves of repeated Muslim
invasions, and many escaping Indian masters came to Tibet.

Around that time the Kadam tradition developed. Although it was
later integrated into the other four schools—Nyingma, Sakya, Kagyu,
and Gelug—originally the Kadam tradition was on its own. Its
founder, the Indian master Atisha, worked tirelessly to reestablish the
teachings and strengthen Buddhism in Tibet by showing there was no
contradiction in practicing both Sutrayana and Vajrayana.

Because Atisha was a Prasangika practitioner, Prasangika views
became prominent in the second dissemination, whereas they had
hardly existed in the first. Around this time, as well, translations of
Buddhist texts into Tibetan were becoming far more accurate. A
translation would be accepted only after there was agreement between
both of the bilingual translators, one Indian and one Tibetan. All the
texts from both the Kangyur (teachings of the Buddha himself) and
the Tengyur (shastras or commentaries) were translated in this way.

Marpa Lotsawa, a contemporary of Atisha who founded the Kagyu
tradition, held Prasangika views. His disciple was Milarepa, who was

famous for his austerity and the many beautiful songs and poems he wrote. Although the Sakya tradition had started much earlier, it really flowered around the same time as the Kagyu tradition, and Sakya Pandita (1182–1251), the greatest philosopher of the Sakya tradition, was also a very strong advocate of Prasangika Madhyamaka views. Later, Lama Tsongkhapa (1357–1419), who championed Chandrakirti's interpretation of Nagarjuna, went on to found the Gelug school.

With this second dissemination of Buddhism, a pattern emerged in that each Tibetan king had his own Buddhist teacher, and whatever view that master held became, by royal decree, the dominant view of the country. Thus, each of the four traditions became more defined. From about the time of the Fifth Dalai Lama (1617–82) until the Chinese invasion in 1959, the Gelug tradition was dominant.

In this way the four traditions of Tibetan Buddhism were founded, each emphasizing different texts and each with slightly different views on reality, but all paying homage to Nagarjuna as the preeminent interpreter of the Buddha's teachings on ultimate truth. And so it has remained until today. Many learned scholars have written commentaries over the years, but no radically different schools of Buddhist thought have emerged since.

# 2 THE BASE AND THE PATH WITHIN THE FOUR SCHOOLS

## The Tibetan System of Study

THE SYSTEM OF MONASTIC STUDY that developed in Tibet required a clear and understandable structure that students of all abilities could follow; hence, the diversity of philosophical views were simplified into what we now call the four schools, showing clearly the ever-increasing subtlety of view that the student needs to understand and assimilate. Also, presenting the various Buddhist views in four succinct schools made it possible for students to approach each school in the same manner, with distinct areas of study.

The study texts begin their presentations of each of the four schools by providing a definition of that school, enumerating the related sub-schools, and examining the etymology of that school and its specific terminology. Then, each section moves into the principal assertions, or tenets, of that school, which are divided into:

+ base
+ path
+ results of the path

The study of phenomenology (the way the mind experiences phenomena) and of ontology (how things exist) are popular subjects in Western philosophy, but they are subjects that are pursued for their own sake. In Buddhism there is no point in studying such things in and of themselves. The purpose of our study is enlightenment, which is the result of a long process of spiritual development, and that development depends on working with things and events as they exist in our world.

The only reason to do anything is to achieve a result—in our case, full enlightenment, the result of the path—and for that we need methods to achieve that result—that is, the path itself. But if our methods are not based on reality, they will flounder. Therefore, it is vital to be aware of how things actually exist, on the one hand, and how we misread reality, on the other, in order to correct our delusions. That is the base. It is the foundation upon which the real work happens. This shows that Buddhism is more than mere abstract philosophy.

Each text surveying the spectrum of philosophical views is organized in this way, from the shortest ten-page overview to the longest thousand-page treatise. In our monastic education, we begin by studying the "lowest" school, the Vaibhashika, according to this outline for an extended period; then we move on to the next school and follow exactly the same structure, and so on. This makes it easy to compare each school with the ones already studied.

## The Base of the Path

The first main section, the base of the path, has the following subdivisions that are studied with each philosophical school. They are:

+ objects—the two truths, etc.
+ object-possessors (i.e., subjects)
  - persons
  - consciousnesses
  - terms

The lower schools tend to place their attention on the objects themselves, without referring to relative and ultimate truth; as a result, their focus is on topics such as the five aggregates, their general characteristics such as impermanence and selflessness, and their specific characteristics such as form, feeling, and so forth. The principal focus of the Mahayana schools' study of the base is the two truths themselves and how they relate. This is done by focusing on the subjective side, although here, the term used for *subject* is actually *object-possessor*. The term *subject* typically refers to a person, whereas *object-possessor* refers to more than just person. When we study the object-possessor, we study three things: *persons*, the concepts of what the self is; *consciousnesses*, the nature of the mind; and *terms*, the way the labels we place on an object also "possess" that object in some way.

This is an interesting point, and one not immediately apparent. Terms "possess" an object in that they are more than mere sounds or letters written on a page. If we name a yellow thing with petals "flower," that object somehow takes on a different meaning to us. With naming, something is added that is beyond the actual existence of the object, so in that way the term "possesses" the object. As we will see later when we examine what is considered the most subtle view, that of the Prasangika Madhyamaka, the nature of any phenomenon, including one's self, is no more than a mere label or term placed on an ever-changing, interdependent base.

Although differentiating subject from object in this way makes for clearer areas of study, it should be noted that object-possessors are in no way outside the realm of the two truths. Anything that is not an ultimate truth is a conventional or relative truth, and this includes persons, consciousnesses, and terms. The separation is not in the mode of existence of the object but in the way we examine them.

## The Two Truths as the Base

Even before the Buddha, Indian philosophers saw that we suffer because we mistake reality. Thus, the search for an understanding of how things exist has always been paramount. For the higher Buddhist schools, this means that we need to understand the two truths.

Each of the two truths is neatly seen as the cause for each of the two aspects of the spiritual path, the practices of method and wisdom. An understanding of relative, or conventional, truth leads to the cultivation of the method side of compassion, ethics, and so on, whereas an understanding of ultimate truth leads to the cultivation of the wisdom side. Finally, when these two aspects have been developed to perfection and the results of the path are realized, the method side becomes the cause of the *form body* of a buddha while the wisdom side becomes the cause of the *truth body*.

| | | |
|---|---|---|
| the two truths (the base): | conventional | ultimate |
| the two practices (the path): | method | wisdom |
| the two buddha bodies (the result): | form body | truth body |

We can see this in the differing aspects of our own lives. We have both an intuitive, emotional aspect and an intelligent, logical aspect. The emotional aspect corresponds exactly to the method side of the path and attaining the buddha's form body (the activities of an enlightened being), whereas the logical aspect corresponds to the wisdom side and the buddha's truth body (the wisdom aspect of an enlightened being).

Our understanding of our world has many layers. As with the skin of an onion, we can peel away the surface appearances and see deeper levels beneath, and this can go on and on, in a process that is seemingly without end. Seeing the color and shape of a flower is one way of relating to that flower's conventional existence, but there are many levels of the modes of existence of that flower. We need to work through these various levels to reach an understanding of the final mode of existence, the *ultimate* truth of the flower. Thus, understanding conventional truths—how phenomena exist and operate on this conventional, worldly level—is the key to understanding how they exist at the deepest level, as ultimate truths. Conversely, misunderstanding the conventional mode of existence will block our understanding of the ultimate mode of existence.

## THE PATH

Just as the base of the path has subdivisions, so does the study of the path. They are:

+ the objects of observation of the path
+ the objects of abandonment of the path
+ the nature of the path

The four noble truths begin with the truth of suffering. We need to start with an understanding of suffering before we can work toward its elimination. Similarly, here we need a firm understanding of the basis of how phenomena exist. Then, by differentiating clearly between suffering and happiness on the basis of this, we will have the tools to reduce our suffering and increase our happiness. Thus, we move from base to path. When the philosophical schools are studied in the monastery, the meaning of the term *path* according to each of the philosophical schools is explained by way of looking at its three subdivisions.

The first subdivision is *the objects of observation of the path*. In the *Four Noble Truths Sutra* the Buddha said that the fourth noble truth, the truth of the path leading to the cessation of suffering, must be cultivated. Here we look at the areas of our practice that we need to develop. This is a vast subject.

It is common in the study of the four noble truths to divide each truth into four aspects, or characteristics. For example, impermanence, suffering, selflessness, and emptiness are the four characteristics of the first truth. These sixteen aspects[4] form the core subject matter for the study of the base, no matter which school we are studying. Attack Buddhist philosophy from any angle, approach it through any school or topic, and sooner or later, we will always come back to the four noble truths and these sixteen characteristics.

An example of this is Maitreya's *Ornament of Clear Realization* (*Abhisamayalamkara*), one of the main texts used in the Gelug tradition. Each of the eight chapters contains one or more of the sixteen characteristics, presented in slightly different ways. Throughout Buddhist literature these sixteen characteristics appear. If your goal is to become a bodhisattva and attain enlightenment, the sixteen characteristics of the four noble truths should be observed in one way; if you are seeking your own liberation, they should be observed in another way. These are the objects of observation in connection with the assertions regarding the base.

Following the objects of observation are *the objects of abandonment*, the obstacles that stand between us and spiritual development. For example, just as impermanence is a key feature in our study of the objects of observation, the ignorance of impermanence is a key hindrance to our development. Logically, we all know we are going to die, but at a deeper level there is some obstacle to fully assimilating this into our mindstream. Ideally we would live our lives with a deep-felt sense of our own impermanence and a sense of the preciousness of each moment, but I suspect we're all a long way from this goal. We instinctively feel that our self is quite permanent, which is a wrong view and an object to be abandoned. It is the same with the other objects of abandonment.

The last of the three subdivisions within the path is *the nature of the path*. In our monasteries this is mainly a study of the various realizations that we need to attain along the path, and is a guide to what the practitioner should be practicing at which level.

## THE RESULTS OF THE PATH

We embark upon a spiritual path in order to achieve a goal. For a Buddhist the goal is enlightenment or liberation. These two wonderful concepts are so easily misunderstood that a great deal of study is needed in order to understand exactly what we are aiming for. While agreeing that these results of the path are the ultimate goal, each philosophical school has its own views on the actual meaning of liberation and enlightenment. This difference in views on the final goal of practice is just one example of how each of the four Buddhist philosophical schools attempts to get at the truth behind the core concepts that the Buddha taught in its own way. So before we take each school in turn, let's take a look at some of those core concepts.

## The Core Concepts of Tibetan Buddhism

### BUDDHIST TENETS

The study of the four philosophical schools is usually referred to as the study of tenets, or tenet systems. Buddhist philosophy is ruthlessly logical, and we must use our sharpest faculty of discernment to determine whether the assertions within Buddhism are in fact true. If something is established as being true, it is a tenet. The Tibetan for *tenet* is a wonderfully precise word, *drubta* (*grub mtha*), *drub* meaning "established" and *ta* meaning "conclusion." *Drubta* literally means an established conclusion. More specifically a tenet is a philosophical conclusion that is reached through analysis and examination and has become incontrovertible in our minds.

At present I might feel that my body is impermanent, but I could never claim that this feeling is a tenet. I certainly don't act like my body is impermanent! If, however, through a long process of analysis, I reach the irrefutable conclusion that it is impermanent, and if that understanding informs everything I do, then that would definitely be a tenet. *Tenet*—established conclusion—refers to making the analysis and then holding the view that results from the conclusion reached. It is to this depth of understanding that Buddhist philosophy aims to bring us.

From the second stage of the development of Buddhism in India onward, much of the debate focused on the most basic tenets of Buddhism: the four seals.[5] The four seals are:

1. All compounded phenomena are impermanent.
2. All contaminated things are suffering.
3. All phenomena are selfless.
4. Nirvana is true peace.

These four statements are what "seal" our minds to the Buddhist path. If we firmly hold these four thoughts as true, we are holders of Buddhist philosophy whether we call ourselves Buddhist or not.

The first seal says: "All compounded phenomena are impermanent." Whether something is a material object or a mental event, whether it is useful or garbage, if that thing is created through causes and conditions—that is, if it is compounded—then it is impermanent. This is a crucial concept in Buddhism.

All Buddhist masters, from the Buddha himself, taught the importance of understanding impermanence. While there is no disagreement about that, understanding exactly what the Buddha meant by *impermanence* has been a huge point of debate, and many different views have grown up about it.

In the statement "All contaminated things are suffering," *contaminated* is the important point here. The world comes into existence due to causes and conditions. If those causes and conditions are in turn the products of a deluded mind, then those resultant things or events are contaminated and will unquestionably cause future suffering. Therefore, they are suffering by definition. No matter how beautiful or valuable a thing might be, it is suffering because it will sooner or later cause difficulties, pain, and misery.

The term *selfless* in the statement "All phenomena are selfless" is one of the most vital concepts in Buddhism, and one that differentiates more than any other the Buddha's philosophy from other existing philosophies. While the core of the non-Buddhist philosophies was *atman*, or self, the Buddha was truly revolutionary in his first teaching by asserting *anatman*, or selflessness. This was a very contentious issue between Buddhist and non-Buddhist philosophers, and in some ways most of the philosophical debates among Buddhists themselves has been an attempt to understand and refine what is meant by selflessness.

With the last "seal," the Buddha taught that a state of true peace—nirvana—is possible. *Nirvana* does not refer to a place or a state of mind but simply to the mere absence of suffering and its causes.

Having an understanding of these four seals and the differing interpretations of their key concepts—being impermanent, contaminated, selfless, and at peace—can act as a handle to allow us to see the gradual evolution of Buddhist thought, as we study the views of different masters who work with the same essential concepts and yet reach quite different conclusions depending on the subtlety of their understanding.

IMPERMANENCE

If all compounded phenomena are impermanent, then what exactly does "impermanent" mean? Of the many different interpretations of the term, we will examine only two. These two appear to be dichotomous ideas; nevertheless, all other views can be seen to fit within these two. They are:

+ Production, abiding, aging, and disintegration occur serially.
+ Production, abiding, aging, and disintegration occur simultaneously.

The first concept is what we would normally, instinctively accept as impermanence. Any object has a cause and hence is produced. That object then remains for a period of time, but sooner or later it ceases to exist. All things arise, abide, and disintegrate. This view was widely held in the second period of Buddhism, the time of King Ashoka.

Dating from much later, the second radically different view of impermanence asserts that the processes that are common to all impermanent things occur simultaneously. Although at a gross level impermanent things appear to arise, abide, and disintegrate sequentially, at a subtler level there is no such sequence. On one level the first view is certainly true, but it suggests that during the time of abiding, the object has a stability that it really does not have. There is no single moment in the existence of an object when it is not in the process of disintegration on a subtle level; at the very moment of coming into existence, it disintegrates. Thus, because the coming into existence and the disintegration are simultaneous, there is no time in which a phenomenon stays static. And so in this second view, impermanence means *changing moment by moment*.

Furthermore, the very same causes and conditions that bring the object into existence also cause it to disintegrate. There are not some causes and conditions that cause it to arise and other causes and conditions that make it disintegrate.

This more refined view is ascribed to Dignaga and his disciple, Dharmakirti. That is not to say that the Buddha did not teach this second notion of impermanence—I'm sure he did—or that it had never been mentioned previously. But these two philosophers really analyzed this view systematically.

When we study the lamrim[6] teachings on impermanence today, there is usually a very practical emphasis on the impermanence of our life—that our death is certain, yet our time of death is uncertain. This is meant to make us aware of how fragile our life is so we don't waste it. The fact that this gross view of impermanence is so strongly emphasized does not mean that seeing impermanence as momentary change is purely abstract philosophy. The grosser understanding is of immediate help for the grosser level of problems we face, but to get to the bottom of our problems, we also need the subtler understanding.

## SELFLESSNESS

While we are usually not mistaken when we view objects on the conventional level, our inability to see their interconnectedness is the cause of all our problems. Seeing objects as concrete, discrete, independent, existing from their own side, without causes, and so on may or may not bring manifest suffering on us right now. This mistaken worldview, however, is dangerous, and never more so than when the object is the sense of self.

The concepts of selfhood that we hold are the main focus of the fifth volume of the *Foundation of Buddhist Thought* series, *Emptiness*, so I will only touch on them here. For a Buddhist practitioner, having a correct concept of the self is probably the most important tool on the path to full awakening.

Both Buddhist and non-Buddhist philosophies in ancient India were based on the idea of karma, or cause and effect. The existing and predominant non-Buddhist schools' doctrine of *atman* asserted a permanent, unitary, and unchanging self that went from life to life. In direct contrast to this, the Buddha expounded the doctrine of *anatman*, or noself. The many centuries during which Buddhist thought developed saw many explanations of what the Buddha meant by *person*, or *self*.

The Buddha does not hesitate to talk as if the person really exists: he uses the common pronouns—I, we, they, and so on—that we all use in conversation. But when actually asked if the "I" exists, he was reticent to answer, knowing how easily a simple yes or no can bring confusion. We work at a conventional, superficial level every day, and at that level, of course the "I" exists. The vast majority of the Buddha's teachings are pitched at this level. They are advice to help us become better people, and in them the Buddha does not hesitate to say "I" and "you." Conventionally, we exist, make mistakes, suffer, and so on. On another level, the substantial, singular, permanent "I" does not exist, and that is what Buddhism challenges.

The "I" is not substantial, nor is it unitary or singular in there being only one "thing" we can point to and say this is our self. And of course the "I" cannot be permanent. Without falling into nihilism, the early Buddhist philosophers refuted the views of the non-Buddhist schools (such as the Samkhya or Brahmanism) that assert just such a permanent, unitary, and indivisible self.

Be careful not to reject non-Buddhist philosophy as naively simplistic because it seems inconceivable to you that any school of thought would believe the self to be unchanging. When you study their philosophies, they are much more subtle than they may initially seem. For them the self is permanent because it continues from life to life, not because it does not change; it is unitary because it is of one nature; and it is indivisible because it is that part of us that is not dependent on causes and conditions. This is *atman*, a concept that is still deeply rooted in Hinduism to this day. The Buddha was being quite revolutionary to go against this belief.

Frankly, I suspect very few of us lead our lives as if we are impermanent and constantly changing. Logically, of course, we accept this idea, but if we were to analyze thoroughly the causes of our problems, we would see that they almost always stem from the clash that exists between the deep-seated sense of an unchanging "I" and the simple fact that it is constantly changing.

Nobody denies that we all have a strong sense of "I." Very few, however, are able to define exactly what is meant by that term. Ask most people and they will point to some indefinite place on their body and say "it's me" or some such thing. Try to pin them down, however, and things become very vague; this "I" that rules our life proves to be very elusive. When we search for it, we can't actually find it, although all of us feel instinctively that it is somewhere within us, either our mind, or our body, or our mind and body together.

Perhaps, due to culture or education or even our own investigation, we might conclude that the sense of self is quite separate from the mind/body collection and is somehow connected to something eternal, such as the soul's connection with God, or the atman's connection with Brahma. There may be great spiritual benefits to holding this view, but it is a hard position to defend against philosophical analysis.

Perhaps we feel the "I" is just our body and mind together. But in that case, if we really check the "I" out, we'll see that almost invariably our "I" appears to be singular and indivisible. This means that it won't work to say "just body and mind," which assumes a collection and hence is multiple, not singular.

We need to explore this. If we are our body and the body is destroyed at death, then the whole notion of karma becomes invalid. Buddhism strongly rejects that the body alone is "I." In the same way, our mind alone, or aspects of our mind, cannot be the "I." For instance, if my memory is me, what would happen to "me" if I lost my memory? Or if my thinking is me, when I'm not thinking, is there no longer me? Descartes' famous "I think, therefore I am" does not hold up to Buddhist analysis.

If there is a real person, Buddhism says, it must have continuity. If it stopped sometimes for whatever reason, then the concept of karma would collapse. There is no way that the action we do today will have a result in the future unless the "I" is in some way continuous.

While all Buddhist schools reject the above notions of self, they each hold their own views about what the self is. The main assertions are:

1. the mere collection of the aggregates
2. an inexpressible reality
3. the continuum of the aggregates
4. the mind-basis-of-all
5. the mental consciousness
6. the mere "I"

At first, *the mere collection of aggregates* might sound as if our "I" is our entire mind and body aggregates collectively, but this word *mere* is important. It means lacking in any substantial existence at all. There is no substantially existent "I" within the various aggregates that are our body and mind. On the other hand, we almost certainly feel that our "I" is substantial in some way.

Another concept of "I" is as *an inexpressible reality*. Here the "I" is viewed as neither one with the aggregates nor separate from them; therefore, although the "I" exists, how it exists is inexpressible.

The third concept, *the continuum of the aggregates*, indicates that the person is not the aggregates but that a sense of self arises due to the stream of consciousness, which in turn is a result of the chain of cause and effect of one moment of consciousness causing the next moment of consciousness. This sense of continuity gives the illusion of a substantially existent "I."

The next view, *the mind-basis-of-all* (Skt. *alayavijñana*), is a very late development in the theories of selfhood. Here the "I" is regarded as the particular mind within our mental existence that holds all the karmic imprints. We will discuss this later in the context of the Chittamatra school.

Another view of person is that it is *the mental consciousness*. From the four mental aggregates, it is not feeling, discrimination, or compositional factors, but purely consciousness.

Finally, there is the notion that the person is *the mere "I."* This is considered to be the most subtle among all the Buddhist views. Here the person is nothing more than a label applied to a valid basis—the ever-changing collection of mind and body. That we misunderstand it as more than just an insubstantial label is a prime cause of our suffering.

If we look historically at all these concepts of person, the first two—*the mere collection of the aggregates* and *an inexpressible reality*—existed from very early on and are held by the Vaibhashika and Sautrantika schools, respectively. The last concept, that of *the mere "I"*—which is the Prasangika view currently held and considered to be correct by most Tibetan Buddhists—also comes from very early on in Buddhist history, from Nagarjuna. *The mind-basis-of-all* was posited by Asanga and Vasubandhu and the Chittamatra school. *The mental consciousness* and *the continuum of the aggregates* come mainly from Bhavaviveka and are views held by the Svatantrika Madhyamaka subschool.

## Arriving at Right View

In his seminal teaching on the four noble truths, the Buddha codifies the fourth truth—the truth of the path—as the noble eightfold path.

From among these eight right practices, one of them is *right view*. Right view can be explained on many different levels: the understanding of cause and effect, of cyclic existence, of the mode of existence of phenomena, and so on. Right view encompasses the whole wisdom side of the Buddha's teachings.

One of the most important aspects of right view is understanding the correct mode of existence of all the phenomena that make up the universe, particularly our sense of identity. You will often find the term *emptiness* (Skt. *shunyata*) used here in Buddhism.

This quest for valid understanding never stops until enlightenment is reached. On the very advanced path of the *bodhisattva*—one who has attained the altruistic mind that spontaneously works for the welfare of others—this is reflected in the practice of what are called the *six perfections*. Each of the first five aspects of the bodhisattva's role—generosity, ethics, patience, joyous effort, and concentration—only becomes a "perfection" contingent on the sixth perfection, the wisdom realizing emptiness. Ethics, for example, are vital, but no matter how ethical we are, unless those ethics rest on a base of right understanding of the nature of reality, they will be flawed.

Without wisdom, the Buddha says, the other perfections are like a blind person, wandering without direction. Wisdom is what channels all our other practices in the right direction, developing the right causes and conditions to experience complete enlightenment, free of delusion and ignorance.

As we look at the different schools of philosophical thought, we will see diverse viewpoints and varying levels of subtlety. It is not like the study of Western philosophy, which seems to me to focus on different views for the sake of intellectual virtuosity alone. These different Buddhist views are incremental stages in the development of a practitioner's understanding of the Buddha's thought and represent increasing degrees of subtlety of view that we must all pass through if we are to progress along the path.

Whatever we do to develop compassion opens the heart; and opening our heart fully comes from opening our eyes, from wisdom. The wish to overcome anger and selfishness is important, but we will never accomplish them without the necessary tool—right view.

# 3 THE VAIBHASHIKA SCHOOL

## The Great Exposition

As I MENTIONED ABOVE, the four Buddhist philosophical schools as presented in the monastic universities were not so neatly demarcated historically. The huge advantage, however, in such a manner of presentation is the clarity and (relative) simplicity that such a structure allows. For that reason, I will follow this structure here.

The first of the schools studied in Tibetan monasteries, the Vaibhashika (Great Exposition) school, takes its name from a text called the *Great Exposition of Particulars* (*Mahavibhasha*), because this school's core assertions on the base, path, and result all come from this text.

As we have seen, the *base* refers to how a particular school perceives the manner of existence of phenomena, the *path* to what should be adopted and what abandoned based on a thorough knowledge of the base, and the *result* to the goal that a practitioner attains by following such a path. Again, this is the standard template used in the monasteries to explain each school.

The *Great Exposition of Particulars* is a thorough presentation of seven Abhidharma texts that the Vaibhashika masters assert were taught by the Buddha. The seven texts are: *Dharmasamgrahani* by Shariputra, *Prajñaptishastra* by Maudgalyaputra, *Prakaranapada* by

Vasumitra, *Jñanaprastan* by Katyayanaputra, *Vijñanakaya* by Devasharma, *Sangitiparyaya* by Mahakaustila, and *Dhatukaya* by Purna.

There have been several attempts to translate the entire *Great Exposition of Particulars* into Tibetan, but unfortunately it is currently only available in Pali and Chinese. Whatever we study about the text is reliant on what subsequent commentators have said about it. Of the seven Abhidharma treatises that make up the text, only two are available in Tibetan.

Generally, we take what we know about this school from Vasubandhu's *Treasury of Higher Knowledge* (*Abhidharmakosha*) and his autocommentary (*Abhidharmakoshabhashyam*). Most of the subsequent writings on this school from Tibetan masters are based on Vasubandhu.

## Divisions of Phenomena

The Vaibhashika school is the first and least subtle of the schools and is largely dismissed by the later schools except as a means of refining their own views. In spite of this, there is one area where Vaibhashika ideas have proved to be not only an excellent primer but also so succinct that their approach has carried through to all the other schools, and that is in the area of the classification of phenomena, where all things and events in the universe are categorized in order to better understand them. Before undertaking an extensive investigation of *how* things exist, it is very useful to be clear about *what* exists in the universe. The basic categories that are presented in this school have been so workable that none of the other schools have been tempted to change them radically. Of course, when it comes to the finer details there are some differences, and some ideas particular to one school are redefined or rejected by another school. But the overall structure and the concepts used in Vaibhashika classification apply for all the schools.

## COMPOUNDED AND UNCOMPOUNDED PHENOMENA

In the Abhidharma texts, existent things are presented in two categories:

+ compounded phenomena
+ uncompounded phenomena

All existent things, both within and outside of cyclic existence, fit into one of these two categories. From them, Vasubandhu's *Treasury of Higher Knowledge* starts with an explanation of uncompounded phenomena, simply because there are significantly fewer divisions. Thus, it is easier to understand and memorize—a very important point for a young monk in a monastery.

Here, *uncompounded* means:

+ something that is not created by the coming together of causes and conditions,
+ something that does not change moment by moment during its existence, and therefore,
+ something that cannot perform a function.

In the *Treasury of Higher Knowledge*, the main examples of uncompounded phenomena are space and the two types of cessation, non-analytical and analytical. *Non-analytical cessation* refers to the temporary ceasing of certain types of negativities, misperceptions, and so on when we enter the meditative concentration that interrupts our attachment to sensory objects. When the concentration stops, our attachment naturally returns. *Analytical cessation* occurs by means of the meditation analyzing the reality of things and events, and is a complete cessation in that there is no reversal. It is the full cessation borne of realization.

*Space* is the mere absence of obstruction; as such it is not the result of any causes and conditions.

The term *compounded phenomena* is a synonym for impermanent phenomena and refers to those things that come into being because of causes and conditions. You will remember the first of the four Buddhist seals discussed above: "All compounded phenomena are impermanent." Vasubandhu defines a compounded phenomenon as:

> ...an object that has arisen in dependence on the aggregation of causes and conditions.[7]

Compounded phenomena, which include all other existent things, can be categorized in many different ways, but the main subdivisions are:

1. form
2. consciousness
3. nonassociated compositional factors

All things and events that come into existence due to causes and conditions can be found within these three subdivisions. Whether they are within samsara or beyond it, whether they should be abandoned or adopted, whether they are external phenomena or internal mental events—anything that comes into existence in dependence on the aggregation of causes and conditions is here.

*Form* does not refer here only to gross material things—shape, color, pen, book, and so forth—but also to any object of the sensory consciousnesses. It thus includes things like odors and sounds as well.

*Consciousness* refers to all mental events. Again, the basic concept of consciousness that the Vaibhashikas assert has proved so useful and unassailable that it has been adopted by all the other schools. This understanding of material and mental phenomena is at the core of any presentation on Buddhist philosophy.[8]

There are six main consciousnesses. The first five are related to the sense organs: sight (eye), hearing (ear), smell (nose), taste (tongue), and touch (body). The sixth is the mental consciousness, in which we can include all sorts of mental processes: thoughts, emotions, intelligence, feelings, and so on, as well as all uncontaminated consciousnesses.

The third category, *nonassociated compositional factors*, refers to all other phenomena that come together due to causes and conditions but don't fit into the other two categories. A classic example of this is an image we see in a dream. Perhaps we have dreamed of a nice beach. Although the dream itself is consciousness, the image that appears in the dream is not consciousness, nor is it form; nevertheless, it is a compounded phenomenon, since it has come into existence due to causes and conditions.

Nonassociated compositional factors also includes abstract phenomena, such as time, continuity, aging, birth, and the very important phenomenon of person. Person—our sense of identity, our "I"—is neither form nor consciousness, and yet it is a compounded phenomenon because it comes into existence due to the aggregation of causes and conditions. All Buddhist schools assert that this is correct.

## The Vaibhashika View of the Two Truths

Since we need to examine each school's explanation of reality and how we generally perceive that reality, we tend to force the Vaibhashika views into the template of the two truths. Unlike the Mahayana schools, however, there is no real comparable presentation of the two truths either in this school or in the next, the Sautrantika, even though the terms "conventional" and "ultimate" are often used in connection with other things.

The main focus of this school's presentation is on the thirty-seven aspects of the path to enlightenment. These thirty-seven are divided into seven groups; they provide a general structure of the entire Buddhist path. To me, the thirty-seven aspects are an integral framework for anyone who is studying Buddhism, since they clearly show what is needed, and at what stage, on the journey to enlightenment. Starting from the first group, the four mindfulnesses, up to the last group, the noble eightfold path, everything about the thirty-seven aspects is related to the four noble truths, and the practices associated with each of the thirty-seven aspects are tools that can take us from where we are now all the way up to enlightenment.[9]

If you are a student of Tibetan Buddhism, it might seem that these practices are not essential, as they are not emphasized in the Tibetan tradition. But in reality, they are vital; they are the basic structure of any Buddhist practice. The six perfections and the four means of drawing students to the Dharma are very advanced and are in addition to these, not substitutes for them.

Although these thirty-seven aspects are the main focus for both the Vaibhashika and Sautrantika schools, their scholars did consider the Buddha's all-important concept of selflessness from the point of view of how we misconceive reality. The two truths are present in their philosophies, albeit implicitly. In the *Treasury of Higher Knowledge*, however, when referring to this school, Vasubandhu uses not only the terms *conventional* and *ultimate*, but also *conventional truth* and *ultimate truth*. From that, we are able to trace back and infer what the Vaibhashikas consider to be the two truths.

In the seventh chapter of the *Treasury of Higher Knowledge*, for example, there is a section about contaminated and uncontaminated consciousnesses. Vasubandhu explains that the objects that appear to a contaminated consciousness are the objects of a conventional mind. He connects these concepts further by showing that a contaminated consciousness refers to the mindstream of a being who has not realized selflessness directly. From this, it can be surmised that conversely, objects of an uncontaminated consciousness—the mind of a being who *has* realized selflessness directly—must be objects of an ultimate mind. In the seventh chapter of Vasubandhu's autocommentary, it says:

> Contaminated things—vase, cloth, person, male, female, and
> so on—
> Such things the contaminated mind apprehends;
> Therefore, it is called a conventional consciousness.[10]

The examples cited by Vasubandhu—vase, cloth, person, male, female—are objects of contaminated consciousnesses because they are conventional objects apprehended by a consciousness that has not realized selflessness directly. In the Vaibhashika presentation, *conventional* generally refers to something that is not true as it appears.

Although the term *truth* is not added, it is implied by the way that *conventional* and *ultimate* are used. Thus, objects are defined depending on whether they are perceived truly or falsely, which in turn depends on whether the mind perceiving them is uncontaminated (hence, correct) or contaminated (hence, faulty). What defines *true* and *false* really depends on the various schools' interpretation, but even here *true* is presented more as ultimate truth and *false* more as conventional truth.

Another verse from the fifth chapter of the *Autocommentary* says:

> The earlier masters assert that objects of supramundane con-
> sciousnesses and of consciousnesses obtained after supramun-
> dane consciousnesses are called ultimate truths.
> Objects apprehended by other consciousnesses are conven-
> tional truths.[11]

By "earlier masters" Vasubandhu is apparently referring to the Vaibhashika masters.[12] It is quite clear from the quote that they assert conventional and ultimate truths from the point of view of mundane and supramundane consciousnesses, which are close, if not synonymous, with contaminated and uncontaminated consciousnesses. Thus, a mundane, contaminated consciousness—one that has not realized emptiness or selflessness—knows conventional truths, whereas a supramundane, uncontaminated consciousness—one that has realized selflessness directly—knows ultimate truths. Similarly, there is a quote from Purnavardhana in his commentary on the *Treasury of Higher Knowledge* that says:

> It is called *ultimate truth* because it is the object of superior wisdom.
> It is the ultimate and it is also true, and therefore, it is called *ultimate truth*.[13]

This kind of usage is very similar to the Madhyamaka presentation. It is clear from all this that the terms *conventional* and *ultimate* are used in many different ways in the texts of the Vaibhashika school.

## CONVENTIONAL TRUTH AND IMPUTED EXISTENCE

Had there been explicit explanations of the two truths in the Vaibhashika writings, I'm sure the later Tibetan masters would have seized them and used them in explaining this school's tenets. As it is, the Tibetan commentators always come back to one particular verse from the sixth chapter of Vasubandhu's *Treasury of Higher Knowledge*, the text that explains the Vaibhashika view of conventional and ultimate truth most clearly:

If the awareness of something does not operate after that thing
Is destroyed or mentally separated into other things,
Then that thing exists conventionally, like a pot or water.
Others exist ultimately.[14]

This is the simplest explanation of conventional truth, but one that nonetheless requires a degree of flexibility in our thinking. It says that when an object is destroyed or mentally separated into parts, the mind can no longer hold on to that object; therefore, it is a conventional truth. For example, if a glass jar is dropped on the floor, it will shatter and no longer be a glass jar. At that moment, the mind that apprehended the glass jar can no longer apprehend it, because it no longer exists.

Vasubandhu also uses the example of water, which is called a "collection" (rather than a "shape" as with objects such as jars). Water has no shape of its own but fits into whatever contains it, such as a glass or a riverbank. When water is confined by riverbanks, we see it as a river, but if the thing that gives the water shape (the banks) is gone, as in the time of a flood, we can no longer perceive the water as a river, and so "river" is a conventional truth.

For mental events, although the object cannot be destroyed, it can be separated into parts. The mind perceiving an hour can break that hour down into minutes and the minutes into seconds; time can be "mentally separated." Therefore, the mind no longer apprehends its original object. Objects that have this quality are called *conventional truths*.

In each of the above examples the whole object is imputed onto its parts—that is, the complete thing is imposed onto what is nothing more than a collection of substantial parts. When those parts are separated, the object can no longer hold as an entity.

Therefore, according to Vaibhashika, these are examples of *imputedly existent objects*. Imputed existence and conventional truth are synonyms. Conversely, as we will see below, if the object is not a collection of substantial parts but is the actual substance that makes up those parts, then it is a *substantially existent object*. Substantial existence and ultimate truth are synonyms.

These two sets of synonyms, imputed existence and conventional truth, and substantial existence and ultimate truth, appear again in the other schools. It is important to understand that the meaning changes from school to school. Whether each school accepts substantial existence is another matter, but each one has its own interpretation of what substantial existence means. We should not regard the meaning described here as valid for any other school.

This category of conventional truth fits with the three types of compounded phenomena we looked at previously: form, consciousness, and nonassociated compounded phenomena. That which can be destroyed is form, and that which can be mentally separated is either consciousness or a nonassociated compounded phenomenon. Whatever the type of compounded phenomenon, if the mind holding it ceases when the object ceases, it is a conventional truth and an imputed object.

This tradition asserts that gross forms and continuities are imputed objects. It provides examples of gross objects—vase, mountain, house, and so on—and of continuities—year, month, week, and so on. These are conventional truths because they are purely imputed onto other things. When the thing onto which they are imputed, as I've said, is physically destroyed, such as when a plate is destroyed, the mind that apprehended it as a plate can no longer operate.

Sometimes the term *collective convention* is used. A house is a collective convention because it comes into existence dependent on all the bits—the bricks, windows, and so on; the mind apprehends the whole house in dependence on all those things. Sometimes the term conventional dependence on others is used. For the mind to apprehend "year," it must depend on the continuity of each of the twelve months, so the mind is unable to apprehend "year" without it being a collection of the twelve months of which it is comprised. This is conventional dependence on others.

The term conventional truth dependent on other substances is also used. The molecules that make up water are not the whole glass of water nor the stream that we apprehend. When the water molecules come together as a glass of water or as a stream, this is a conventional truth dependent on other substances.

## Ultimate Truth and Substantial Existence

After the three lines that describe conventional truth, Vasubandhu merely states, "Others exist ultimately." This is elaborated on in his autocommentary, where it says:

> Other than those are the ultimate truths, because even if the mind is separated from the object, such as when [the object] is destroyed, the mind apprehending it still operates, for example, the mind apprehending form.[15]

Other here refers to anything that cannot be destroyed or mentally separated into other things. This is ultimate truth according to this school, and as we have seen, ultimate truth is synonymous here with substantially existent.

What can't be broken down? There are three main categories:

1. the aggregates
2. uncompounded phenomena
3. substantial particles (of matter or mind)

For this school, although the actual aggregation—the collection of parts that make up an object—can be separated further and further, the aggregate itself—form, feeling, consciousness, and so on—cannot. The Vaibhashikas differentiate between the aspect of having form and the form itself.

A body is made of a collection of parts, which are further made up of collections of particles. But body, parts, and particles are all form. If you break the congregation of particles up into smaller groups, the large congregation is destroyed, but it is still form. As the object is progressively broken up, the mind apprehending the various levels of congregation is cancelled, but the mind apprehending form is never destroyed.

Take the previous example we used in the discussion of conventional truth: the glass jar. A glass jar has a nature as a jar; it also has a nature of being form. As a glass jar it is a conventional truth, but as form it is an ultimate truth, because even if the jar is shattered by a hammer and the mind that apprehends the jar can no longer operate, thousands of small pieces exist that are still form, and that form is something that the mind can still apprehend. The mind that apprehended the glass jar as a glass jar is cancelled, but the mind that apprehends form still operates because form can never be cancelled.

Form exists substantially because in order to exist it does not depend on other substances. And form exists ultimately because no matter how much you cut it into pieces, it will still stay as form.

Feeling is another example. Whether we consider a feeling of great pain or just a subtle pain, whether it is pain that lasts for a long time or a short duration, all of these instances are still feeling and cannot be broken down.

The feeling of happiness is a conventional truth because as a specific mental event it must have a duration, and that duration, whether long or short, can be divided into shorter periods. No matter how long that happiness lasts, however, it is still feeling and that is an ultimate truth. All these collections—form, feeling, and so on—are ultimate truths because the individual aspects of that phenomenon can be separated into parts, but the actual overall collection can never be.

From this school's point of view, both conventional truth and ultimate truth coexist within one object. The body is a conventional truth and the body as form is an ultimate truth.

For this school, *uncompounded phenomena*, such as the cessation of suffering or space—the mere absence of obstruction—substantially exist and are, therefore, ultimate truths because their existence does not depend on other things and they do not change while they exist.

Substantial objects are also ultimate truths. Here, however, *substantial* does not mean "made of substances" but the actual substance itself. For this school it means the fundamental building block of the universe, called the *partless particle*, or in the case of mental events, the *partless moment of consciousness*. We will discuss these further below. They are ultimate truths because they cannot be destroyed or further reduced, and the mind that apprehends these partless particles or partless moments will never be stopped. They are substantially existent because their existence is not dependent on other substances.

## ULTIMATE TRUTH, SELFLESSNESS, AND EMPTINESS

In order to refute the non-Buddhists' concept of the self as permanent, unitary, and indivisible, Vaibhashikas assert that the self cannot exist as a different entity from the mind/body aggregates. In the same way that the body is imputed onto the substantially existing particles that make it up, the sense of "I" is imputed onto the mind/body aggregation.

The Vaibhashika understanding of the nature of self goes only as far as the selflessness of person; this is the extent of their emptiness.

They do not talk about the other type of emptiness that we find in the higher schools, the emptiness of other phenomena, such as body, house, and car. At this level, the term *emptiness* refers only to the person being empty of a permanent, unitary, and indivisible reality.

For the Vaibhashika school, emptiness is an ultimate truth. These are not synonyms, however—ultimate truths are not necessarily emptinesses. For Vaibhashikas, there are other ultimate truths within the compounded phenomena—form, feeling, and so on, or the fundamental building blocks of matter, or the shortest moments of consciousness. They assert all these as ultimate truths, but of course they are not emptinesses.

The seventh chapter of the *Treasury of Valid Knowledge* says: "Emptiness and selflessness are two to be entered into [i.e., realized]." It is clear from that statement that even though the Vaibhashikas use the term *emptiness*, it means something different here than it does in the context of the later schools. This, the simplest explanation of emptiness in Buddhism, accords with the meaning of emptiness found in the *Four Noble Truths Sutra*.

## Partless Particles and Partless Moments of Consciousness

The first two realist schools (Vaibhashika and Sautrantika) assert that there are substantially, truly existing objects. As we have seen, a glass jar is not substantially existent but is imputed onto something that is. The quest for what substantially exists was one of the prime foci of the Vaibhashika scholars. In searching for the mode of existence of phenomena, they sought some sort of fundamental particle that serves as the basic building block for all other things. It was only the later, more subtle philosophies that argued that an assertion of any intrinsically existent phenomenon at all is basically flawed.

If we enter for a moment the mind of a Vaibhashika scholar of two thousand years ago, we would be earnestly searching for the primal particle from which all else derives. An object is made of parts, and those parts are made of parts. Logically, then, following this line of investigation, we *must* come to an endpoint, where we will have gone as far as we can, and where we find a particle that can no longer be broken down.

Even though this basic building block may be partless, Vaibhashika scholars assert that it must nevertheless be made of different constituents in order for the myriad objects of this universe to be formed. There must exist within each partless particle the potential for the different elements that constitute our universe: earth, water, fire, and air. These are not the gross elements that we would generally associate with the names, but the aspects of firmness, moistness, heat, and movement. The Vaibhashikas also considered that these partless particles must have within them the potential to be experienced, so they must contain the sense objects of visual form, tactile form, smell, and taste. (It's interesting that sound is not included. The early Buddhist schools, like the Greeks, regarded sound as a wave and therefore not among the components that make up material things.)

Therefore, in the desire realm (the realm we live in), said the Vaibhashikas, partless particles are made of eight constituents: earth, water, fire, and air, and visual form, tactile form, odor, and taste. Buddhism also asserts other realms, so they determined that partless particles in the form realm, where there are only limited senses, have six constituents: earth, water, fire, and air, smell, and taste.

It might seem strange to a Western scientific mind that experiential factors such as touch, smell, and taste are included in the constituents that make up the universe's fundamental particle. This stems from the very basic Buddhist doctrine of karma, which states that if the cause does not have the potential to bring the result, then it is impossible for that result to arise. Therefore, for a partless particle to be experienced in whatever way we experience it—as a car, a hamburger, a stick of incense—there needs to be within that particle the potential to be experienced by the senses. If these fundamental building blocks of external objects do not possess the potential to produce smell, then no matter how much we try, smell cannot be produced.

In the same way that they posited that the smallest form of matter must be the partless particle, the early Vaibhashika philosophers posited a similar fundamental building block of mental events, the *partless moment of consciousness.*

Our consciousness is a stream. I can have a memory of my time at Sera Monastery that flows like a sequence from a movie. Within that there are smaller "scenes" of the memory, and within that there are moments of time remembered. There are still smaller moments of time within that stream of consciousness, and just as with material phenomena, argue the Vaibhashika scholars, there must logically come a point where those moments of consciousness can no longer be broken down—the partless moment of consciousness. Our consciousness is an aggregation of these moments.

The debate between the Vaibhashikas and the other schools is not about whether a partless particle can be further divided but whether the fundamental constituents of the particle, such as the earth and water elements, can stand by themselves without relying on the other elements. Vaibhashika scholars say that the partless particle is the smallest unit of matter or mind and, hence, is indivisible. Scholars of the other schools contend that the elements (earth, fire, and so on) that constitute a partless particle are themselves constituents of that particle, and that in itself makes the particle divisible. In this way, the whole concept of partless particles is called into question.

This is a very rarefied argument, and the other schools see something utterly illogical in the Vaibhashika stance. If, they ask the Vaibhashikas, these smallest units of matter have no parts, which implies no sides or directions and so on, then it stands to reason that two particles would take up no more room than just one. Either these particles have sides and are "atoms" as we would know them, or they are partless and without sides. In this case, there could be no spatial relationship wherein the left side of one particle would touch the right side of another. That being so, two particles would take up the same space as one, as would three, one hundred, one million, and so on. An object, which supposedly consists of millions of these partless particles, would itself take up no more space than one particle. Therefore, the other schools argue, it is impossible for matter to be built from such fundamental partless particles.

This is how it must appear to the modern, logical, scientific mind. Don't forget, however, that these concepts were being formulated in the early centuries of the first millennium. Those who formulated them must have been very astute to devise such sophisticated philosophical arguments. These concepts brought the practitioners who worked with them a long way toward an understanding of reality. It may seem illogical that a Vaibhashika scholar wouldn't concede the point to a Prasangika scholar when confronted with the inconsistencies. But in the first place, such a confrontation probably never took place. And in the second, think about the way that scientists resisted similar assertions made by quantum physicists.

As the formulation came along later, the two truths—relative and ultimate—are not explicit in the Vaibhashika teachings. Nonetheless, the seeds of understanding are there as Vaibhashika proponents strived to explain how the universe exists and how we misperceive it. Relying on Vasubandhu's interpretation of the tenets of the Vaibhashika school, however, we can see that there are unstated assumptions that we can take to be their own two truths: that conventional existence—that is, the world seen from the point of view of a contaminated or mundane consciousness—is imputed existence, and that ultimate existence—that is, the world seen from the point of view of an uncontaminated or supramundane consciousness—is substantial existence.

It is very helpful for us to understand as clearly as possible this school's ideas of the two truths, particularly with regard to substantial and imputed existence, for then we will see how much misperception we have in our daily lives when we encounter compounded phenomena—in other words, all the things and events we encounter in our everyday lives. We impute substantial reality onto compounded phenomena all the time and create suffering for ourselves as a result. Studying this school will help us to reflect on the many misperceptions we hold, and by seeing clearly at this relatively simple level, we can start to reduce those misconceptions and the difficulties that they create for us.

# 4 THE SAUTRANTIKA SCHOOL

## The Sutra School

THERE IS LITTLE DEFINITE INFORMATION on the second school, the Sautrantika, but it seems that the views attributed to it existed quite early on in the development of Buddhist philosophy. It is even unclear what specifically constitutes Sautrantika tenets as opposed to those of the Vaibhashika school. Consequently, a Sautrantika scholar (if there were such a person) reading the words that the Madhyamaka masters put in his mouth might be quite surprised. If he were a modern Sautrantika, he might even sue for libel! Nonetheless, the clear and simple divisions that we use as study guides are vital as we refine and sharpen our ideas about the meaning of reality.

Traditionally, it is said that over time, the views of the Vaibhashika school became more diverse, causing it to divide into eighteen different subschools; it seems that the Sautrantika school arose as a continuation of one of these subschools. There are different assertions about the origins of the school, but it is generally felt that the break came because the scholars who would come to form the nucleus of Sautrantika thinking refuted the Vaibhashika claim that the seven Abhidharma texts they used were actual sutras, counterclaiming that they were in fact just *shastras*, that is, commentaries by later Indian masters.

Within this school there are traditionally two divisions, the *Satran-tikas Following the Sutra*, whose views are very similar to those of the Vaibhashikas, and the *Sautrantikas Following Reason*, whose views are somewhat different. What follows is an examination of what later Buddhist masters describe as the views of the *Sautrantikas Following Reason*.

The name *Sautrantika* itself is a derivation of "sutra." This school is so called because it claims to follow the sutras closely, as opposed (it says) to the Vaibhashika school's reliance on various shastras. Just which sutra the Sautrantikas follow is by no means clear. Some Tibetan historians such as Taranatha (1575–1634) suggest that it is the *King of Prayers Sutra*, whereas others have named other sutras, none of which has been translated into Tibetan. There are not even any texts in the Tengyur (the commentaries in the Tibetan canon) that are attributed to the Sautrantika school.

We mainly take the Sautrantika assertions on the base, path, and result from Dharmakirti's *Commentary on [Dignaga's "Compendium on] Valid Cognition"* (*Pramanavarttika*). Within the Gelug tradition of Tibetan Buddhism, this treatise on Buddhist epistemology and logic is regarded as vitally important. Although Dharmakirti only alludes to the Sautrantika view, when we study Sautrantika tenets in the monastery, we assume that the view provided by Dharmakirti in this seminal text is that of the Sautrantikas, especially when he uses exam-ples of the attributes of the four noble truths and the historical Bud-dha as illustrations of what is "valid." It should be noted, however, that this does not mean that Dharmakirti and Dignaga necessarily held Sautrantika views themselves; their own views tended more toward those of the Chittamatrins.

We can also surmise this school's view from the texts composed by Madhyamikas in which they describe the Sautrantika stance in order to reject it.

The path and the result asserted by the Sautrantikas differ very little from the Vaibhashika presentation, and so we will barely consider them in this section. As with the Vaibhashikas, the path mainly deals with the thirty-seven aspects of the path to enlightenment, and the result is considered to be liberation instead of the full enlightenment as presented by the later schools. For that reason both the Vaibhashika and Sautrantika schools are regarded as individual liberation seekers' schools.

It is this school's assertions about the base that are especially significant. The prominence of Dharmakirti's *Commentary on Valid Cognition* within the Gelug study of this school is due to its comprehensive approach to epistemology and logic. The study of the Sautrantika school is crucial because, even though the later schools reject certain assertions, they nonetheless use the Sautrantika school's epistemological and logical tools.

On our spiritual journey, we need to move from conceptual knowledge to direct experience of the subjects we are studying. The mechanics of how we accomplish this are the key points of the Sautrantika presentation: what conceptual and perceptual consciousnesses are, how they operate, and how we move from conceptualization to direct perception. These topics constitute the major part of the base as asserted by the Sautrantikas.

## Existent Objects

### THINGS AND NONTHINGS

The phenomena that exist in our universe are the base studied by this school. The base is the material that we work on in order to develop the path so that we can achieve the result. If we have a clear idea of the base, it makes our path so much easier. As our object of practice, the base is the four noble truths with the sixteen characteristics. But in order to understand the base at a logical level, the Sautrantikas focus on what exists.

Like the Vaibhashikas, the Sautrantikas are realists in that they assert true independently existing phenomena and that things and events are made up of aggregations of fundamental atoms, i.e., part-less particles and partless moments of consciousness. Thus, the Sautrantikas argue that objects exist intrinsically or inherently and that existent objects can be divided into two.

In the third chapter of his *Commentary on Valid Cognition*, Dharmakirti states that there are two types of valid cognition and therefore there are also two types of existent objects. Here, we have the Sautrantika definition of what exists: it is that which is apprehended by a valid cognition.

A valid cognition, as the name implies, is a mind that apprehends its object validly or correctly. There are two types of valid cognition: direct valid cognitions, which cognize their object directly, such as an eye consciousness seeing a flower; and inferential valid cognitions, which get at their object through inference, such as inferring fire from seeing smoke. From these two kinds of valid cognition there are two kinds of existent objects:

+ things
+ nonthings

Here we define the existence of an object from an epistemological perspective. An object that is apprehended by a direct valid cognition is a *thing* (Skt. *bhava*; Tib. *ngöpo*), whereas an object that is apprehended by an inferential valid cognition is a *nonthing* (Skt. *abhava*; Tib. *ngö may*). Both thing and nonthing exist because they are objects of valid cognitions. If an object is not apprehended by either type of valid cognition, then by definition it is nonexistent.

Nonthings are existent objects that are conceptually constructed. That does not mean that all conceptually constructed objects exist. So in order to differentiate between conceptually constructed objects that exist and those that do not, we need to clarify the notion of "valid" cognition.

The traditional examples of nonexistent objects are space flowers or the horns of a rabbit. Both of these are sheer fantasies and are therefore not objects of valid cognitions, direct or inferential. A more important example is the non-Buddhist concept of *atman*, or self, which, for Dharmakirti and this school, does not exist since it cannot be apprehended by either type of valid cognition, direct or inferential. A follower of the Samkhya school or of Brahmanism might believe in *atman*, but if he were to explore the concept with valid cognition, he would see that it doesn't actually exist.

Objects of conceptual minds that *do* exist are the objects of valid inferences. Imagine an elephant standing on the table where you are currently sitting. Of course, that elephant does not exist. However, for this school, if you consider the nonexistence of that elephant, the *absence of elephant* is an existent object. The difference is that the horns of a rabbit are not an object of a *valid* inferential cognition, whereas thinking of the absence of an elephant on the table (where there is no elephant) is a valid mind. Therefore, the absence of elephant exists. It might seem absurd to ponder whether the absence of an elephant on a table exists or not, but of course this has the deepest relevance when we take it further and explore the status of the "I," which at all levels of Buddhist thought is understood to be selfless.

These two types of existent objects, things and nonthings, correspond quite closely to the division of phenomena that we saw earlier in the Vaibhashika school, into compounded and uncompounded phenomena. They further correspond to another very important division:

specifically characterized and generally characterized phenomena. Things are specifically characterized phenomena, and nonthings are generally characterized phenomena.

## SPECIFICALLY CHARACTERIZED AND
## GENERALLY CHARACTERIZED PHENOMENA

Subjectively—from the point of view of the apprehending mind—a thing is an object of a direct valid cognition, but objectively—from the point of view of the object itself—a thing is a specifically characterized phenomenon, in that it has unique properties not shared by any other object. Conversely, a nonthing is an object of an inferential valid cognition and a generally characterized phenomenon, in that it is a conceptual construct. As such, it is what is called a meaning generality, an image reconstructed by the conceptual consciousness from a collage of images for the purpose of bringing the object to mind.

A specifically characterized phenomenon is unique and is perceived directly by the mind without an intermediary. A generally characterized phenomenon is something the mind characterizes with a generality. I see a car. The specific car that the eye perceives is a specifically characterized phenomenon, but the later memory of the car, or the "car-ness" of the car that the conceptual mind immediately overlays on the perception, is the generally characterized phenomenon.

The definition of a specifically characterized phenomenon is:

a phenomenon realized directly by the mind taking the phenomenon's unique characteristic as its appearing object.

From this we can see that the object must be apprehended by our direct perception, not by our conceptual consciousness, and what the mind apprehends is the unique characteristics of the object, not the general properties that it shares with other objects of the same type. This is crucial, but it is not something that we intuitively and immediately understand.

Here we come back to the two groups of phenomena that make up our external world—those we perceive directly and those we conceptualize. A specifically characterized phenomenon is only apprehended by direct perception, a generally characterized phenomenon only by conception.

When I teach in London, the people who set up the meditation room generally put a glass of water and a small vase of flowers on my table. The vase is made of clear glass and is about the same size and shape as the water glass, although it has a small neck. When I look at these two objects, I invariably think what good examples of specifically and generally characterized phenomena they make. They both look pretty much the same, but because they serve different functions, we give them different names and on one level see them as different. We also, however, unconsciously attribute to them a sameness that they don't actually have.

The water glass is the water glass. It is utterly unique. There is no other water glass that shares exactly those parts and features. That's not to say that there are no other water glasses in the world, but there are no other water glasses that share the same atoms and parts as this one. In that way, this water glass is very specific, and the mind that directly perceives it perceives a specific thing.

Our minds, however, always overlay something extra. The glass vase next to the water glass looks the same in that it is about the same shape and size and it is made of clear glass. As a result, the mind attributes "glass-ness" to it, in terms of its material. What's interesting is that because of its slightly different shape—the small neck—we immediately designate it as "vase," not "water glass," based on what we impute its function to be. Although this is more specific than "thing made of glass," it is still a generalization. There are millions of vases, and we are conceiving this object in that category.

Do you see the difference? The eye perceives something unique—the specific object in front of me—which is the specifically characterized phenomenon, but then the mind overlays this with the generalization of the object's category—"water glass" or "vase"—and this is the generally characterized phenomenon.

Two glasses might even share identical features, but they are still not the same object. So when you perceive glass A, you perceive glass A—its uniqueness. The same is true of glass B. It is the conceptual mind that attributes the commonality to the two different objects.

According to the Sautrantikas, we cannot get at a specifically characterized phenomenon through words. As soon as we use words, we have fallen into generality.

Imagine that you have just returned from the most wonderful holiday of your life. Your mind relives every second of that holiday in vivid detail. Can you say that you are having a direct perception of the whole holiday? Of course not. It is just a memory and, no matter how vivid, an imperfect and incomplete one at that. This is what the Sautrantika scholars are saying here—that words are, by definition, linguistic signs that allow us to mark objects only approximately so that we can make sense of our world.

## REAL AND UNREAL EXISTENT OBJECTS

We can further refine our definition of existent objects. Whether an existent phenomenon is considered to be real or unreal depends on whether it can perform functions. Things are real because they can perform functions that can bring about "real" results, whereas non-things are unreal because they are unable to perform functions.

In the first chapter of Dharmakirti's *Commentary on Valid Cognition* it says:

> Because all [real] things essentially abide in their own essence, they partake in the differentiation between [themselves and the other] similar and dissimilar things.[16]

By analyzing this quotation, we can see that real specifically characterized phenomena can be determined by three criteria. These are:

1. place-specific
2. cause-specific
3. time-specific

They are *place-specific* in that they occupy a definite, special location. I have a table in front of me. It has a specific shape and mass and occupies a specific location. Nothing else can occupy the exact space displaced by the table.

Conceptual images are different. I can imagine the same table, but it occupies no actual location; it is constructed solely in the mind. As such, it is an unreal thing, and generally characterized in this instance because it cannot occupy a definite specific location.

The second criterion is *cause-specific*. In other words, real specifically characterized phenomena come into existence due to specific causes and conditions, unlike generally characterized phenomena, which are conceptually constructed. The mind imagining a particular object of course has causes and conditions, but they are not the specific causes and conditions that brought the object into existence.

And real, specifically characterized phenomena are *time-specific* in that they are locked into a specific time frame, coming into and going out of existence at specific moments due to causes and conditions. Conceptually constructed objects, on the other hand, do not have that kind of clearly determined time and duration. My last trip to India started on a specific day and ended on a specific day, whereas I can recall that trip to mind any time I want. This is the meaning of the words "abide in their own essence" in the quotation. A specifically characterized phenomenon abides in its own essence in the sense that it is not mixed with other things, either in location (because nothing else can share the space it occupies) or causes (in that it has unique causes and conditions that are responsible for its properties and duration) or time frame (where it alone arises when it does and for as long as it does).

For Dharmakirti, an object that conforms to these three criteria is real. It is also an object of perception. "Perception" and "direct valid cognition" are very similar, although not all perceptions are valid. Wrong perceptions can occur, although they tend to be temporary, such as seeing the white snow on a mountain as blue because we are wearing sunglasses, or seeing people on a railway platform in motion when it is actually our train that is moving.

A *thing* has additional properties as well. Because of having these three characteristics and the ability to perform functions (which is also called being effective), a thing therefore possesses its own unique essence and is impermanent.

Because a *nonthing* does not possess these three features, it is unreal, it cannot function (hence, is noneffective), and is permanent.

This is an interesting aspect of the Sautrantikas' notion of generally characterized phenomena that separates them from the Vaibhashikas. A generally characterized object is an imputation (as we have seen), and that, say the Sautrantika scholars, means it is permanent. This conflicts with the Vaibhashika idea of permanence, where there are only three examples of permanent phenomena: the two types of cessation and space. According to the Sautrantika view, there are countless permanent phenomena. All concepts, which by definition do not perform a function, are permanent.

Concepts include inferential valid cognitions as well as all the other nondirect minds, many of which are quite deluded. Deluded or not, there is *always* some degree of distortion of objects that appear to the conceptual mind; such objects may seem real, but they are not. For example, every day I see the large Buddha statue in Jamyang Centre's main meditation room. If, when I am back in my livingroom, I imagine that statue, the image may be vivid and appear to be a real statue to my conceptual mind, but it is not. It is an image of the statue, composed of a distillation of all the images of the statue that I have stored in my mind from all the times I have seen it. Thus, not only is it unreal, it is a generality. That image is a generally characterized phenomenon.

Finally, a *thing*, which has all these aspects, is also an ultimate truth, whereas a nonthing is a conventional truth.

To sum up existent objects according to the Sautrantika school:

| things | nonthings |
|---|---|
| real | unreal |
| functioning | nonfunctioning |
| effective | noneffective |
| specifically characterized phenomena | generally characterized phenomena |
| objects of direct valid cognition | objects of conceptual valid cognition |
| ultimate truths | conventional truths |

We can explore each of the various characteristics listed above under "things" as well as those listed under "nonthings" and thereby come closer to grasping the meaning of ultimate truth and conventional truth, respectively, for the Sautrantikas. Something is real because it functions; something is a specifically characterized phenomenon because it is an object of a direct valid cognition. Something is effective because it functions and is therefore a specifically characterized phenomenon. We can rove around the list, seeing the logical connections between the various terms and in this way clarify the distinctions between ultimate truths and conventional truths in Sautrantika.

## The Relationship of Mind and Object

The Sautrantika school asserts that real things exist really, independent of the mind. This will be refuted by the next school, the Chittamatra, so it is useful to examine the Sautrantika assertions about how something is apprehended by consciousness. Our commonsense view of objects is that they exist out there, in and of themselves, and that a mind completely separate from them apprehends them. This is the Sautrantika view.

External things exist independent of the mind; not only that, they act as a cause for consciousness to arise. By definition, the mind is clear and knowing. In order to know, it must know *something*, so when an eye consciousness sees a flower, the flower is one of the main conditions for a perception of the flower to arise.

There are three conditions needed for consciousness to operate. They are:

1. the object condition
2. the empowering condition
3. the preceding condition

The *empowering condition* is the sense organ that operates to cause a consciousness to arise.[17] The *preceding condition* is the preceding moment of consciousness that allows the next moment of consciousness to arise. For example, in the case of my eye consciousness apprehending a flower, the consciousness operating in the moment prior to the first moment of apprehending the flower is the preceding condition.

The main point in this context, however, is the *object condition*. For me to see a flower, there must be a flower there. It is a real, independent object, existing as a flower there on the table, whether my mind apprehends it or not. When I look at the flower, my eye consciousness—an unmistaken direct perception—apprehends a flower, and therefore, the flower is the object condition.

Since this is a causal relationship, it also has a temporal aspect, in that the flower is the cause and as such precedes the mind that apprehends it, which is the result.

## THE REALITY OF MATERIAL OBJECTS

The early Buddhist philosophers were probing the boundaries between reality and fiction. For the Vaibhashika school, partless particles exist ultimately, but so too do our aggregates, whereas the person, a collection of the body/mind aggregates, does not.

The Sautrantika scholars wanted to refine this, so they designated different sizes of phenomena in order to establish the dividing line between what exists ultimately and what is mere convention. The four levels they hypothesized were:

1. substantial atoms
2. larger molecules
3. collections
4. gross objects

*Substantial atoms* are partless particles. A group of atoms makes a *larger molecule*, and when these become apprehensible—shape and color visible to the eye, smell perceptible to the nose—that is a *collection*. When a collection forms an entire object, that is designated as a *gross object*.

When does an object become a gross object? Is the table a gross object because it is a collection of legs and top? Are the legs a gross object? Scholars disagree. Some say that when color and shape and the other aspects of smell, taste, and touch come together, then that is a gross object.

This subject takes on relevance when we try to separate ultimate truth from conventional truth. For the Sautrantikas, an ultimate truth is an object of direct perception, is substantial, and is able to perform a function, whereas a conventional truth is an imputation that is insubstantial and unable to perform a function. Where is the line drawn on the list of levels of existence that delineates exactly where things become imputed and hence are no longer ultimate truths?

To the Sautrantikas, a person is a conventional truth because of being imputed on the aggregates and unable to perform a function. It is the aggregates of body and mind that perform the functions.

At the other extreme are the substantial atoms, those smallest particles that have substance. Are they real? All the Sautrantika scholars would agree that they are. They are the things that perform functions and that cannot be imputed by a conceptual consciousness. Remember, according to the two lowest schools there must be something that is real and that is the base upon which all else is built. This is the reason why these substantial atoms were inferred, in a way similar way to how scientists "discovered" quarks and neurons.

Though these two lower schools share many aspects, they are not identical in either their emphasis or their assertions. Even in the idea of partless particles there is a difference, with the Sautrantika school asserting that these are comprised of the four elements alone—earth, water, fire, and air—and do not include the sense objects of visual form, tangibility, smell, and taste asserted by the Vaibhashikas.

If gross objects are conventional truths and substantial atoms are ultimate truths, then what about the other two—larger molecules and collections? Logically, collections do not exist from their own side because they rely on larger molecules; likewise, larger molecules do not exist from their own side because they rely on substantial atoms. From this, it might seem that there is no argument and that only substantial atoms are ultimate truths. There are, however, scholars within this school who see larger molecules as some sort of integrated whole and hence "real." They maintain that the dividing line is at collections, which are imputed onto molecules. Still others see "real" as extending all the way up to gross objects.

Although Dharmakirti does not state a clear view on this, he does suggest that commonsense objects such as tables are real, and hence ultimate truths, because our direct perception can cognize them. But he floats between the arguments, depending on whether he is talking from an ontological perspective, where he argues that only substantial atoms are ultimate truths, or from an epistemological perspective, where he presumes gross objects to be real and hence ultimate truths. Epistemologically, perceptions manage to apprehend their objects accurately, thus the objects are real.

So what is "real" according to this school? One viewpoint is that a real object is something that *never changes* and *is not imputed by a conceptual consciousness*. If something is merely imputed by a conceptual consciousness, then Sautrantika scholars say it is not real. That seems to suggest that only substantial atoms are real, as everything else can be imputed onto them.

Another viewpoint, however, suggests that *whatever is perceived by a sense consciousness is real*, whereas anything else is not. Therefore, colors and shapes, tastes, tactile data, and so on, are real, but the objects made up from those things are imputed on them and so are not real.

A third viewpoint is that commonsense objects—houses, tables, pens—are real because they are not constructed by a conceptual consciousness.

So these are the three possibilities, three slightly different views all held by the Sautrantika masters. It is interesting to remember that much of this was debated in an environment of great philosophical ferment. At the time of these debates, there were many views besides Buddhist ones being propagated. One of the strongest was the Samkhya school's idea that not only is the partless particle real, but within the partless particle there is some kind of unifying principle that gives it identity. From the early Buddhist point of view nothing is completely separate from the fundamental building blocks, the atoms.

For Gelug students studying this school—and I am firmly a Gelugpa, as that was my whole monastic grounding—it seems illogical not to take the third stance when looking at this school: that commonsense objects are real because they are not mere imputations of a conceptual consciousness. Let's explore this concept.

According to this argument, commonsense objects are real because they are objects of direct perceptions and are therefore free of constructions or interpretations. The eye sees a book and it is as simple as that, so of course the book is "real." The book is a collection—of parts, color, shape, tangibility, and so on—and each part of that collection is real, so the whole must be real.

But, the counterargument goes, for the book to be real, it must be intrinsic and not rely on other things, whereas it relies on its parts and the label. I am a monk. Am I a real monk? According to this argument I would need to be intrinsically monkly, whereas of course me being a monk depends on other factors: having taken ordination, keeping monks' vows, and so on.

You can see that reality is not a concise thing. If something is real, it must stand by itself, and thus we have a lot of discussion on where the dividing line is between something clearly "standing by itself" and blurring into a mere projection.

## Ultimate Truth and Conventional Truth

### Ultimate Truth in Sautrantika

The basic definition of ultimate truth in Sautrantika is:

> a phenomenon that exists from its own side, without being imputed by a conceptual consciousness.[18]

If you have studied Madhyamaka philosophy before, please leave what you have heard on a shelf for the time being. These lower schools are much more basic, and for them some things do exist from their own side. The quest is to establish the boundary between the intrinsic and the conceptual, so "without being imputed by a conceptual consciousness" tells us that this definition is pointing to the intrinsic, the inherent. If something is imputed by a conceptual consciousness, we take it to mean that it depends on something else, whereas an ultimate truth does not.

Does a computer exist from its own side, without being imputed by a conceptual consciousness? The Sautrantika system says no; it depends on the parts that make it up, whether at the level of screen, hard drive, and so on, or at the deeper level of partless particles. Therefore, it is imputed by a conceptual consciousness in that the mind labels the collection of parts as "computer." This "computer-ness" does not come from the side of the object at all. Furthermore, this concept we see as a complete computer cannot perform a function. It is the actually existing parts that do that. For all these reasons, the computer is a conventional truth. This ties in with the Sautrantika definition of conventional truth:

> a phenomenon that is established as a mere imputation by a conceptual consciousness.[19]

Another explanation of ultimate truth appears in the third chapter of the *Commentary on Valid Cognition*, where Dharmakirti says:

> Those [phenomena] which are able to perform a function are here [said to be] ultimately existent. Others are said to be conventionally existent. Those two [types of phenomena are] specifically and generally characterized.[20]

Although there is some debate about whether this quote represents the actual definition of ultimate and conventional truth within the Sautrantika system, most scholars use it to show exactly what this school sees as the two truths.

As we can see from the first line, phenomena that are able to perform a function are said to be ultimately existent. Here "ultimately existent" is synonymous with ultimate truth. We have already seen that only things that come into existence through causes and conditions are able to perform functions and produce results; such phenomena can also be said to have substantial reality or substance. There are many different connotations, but here *substance* (Tib. *dzay*; Skt. *dravya*) refers to a momentary thing or event that is causally effective in any particular time or circumstance. Those things are ultimate truths because they are able to perform functions to bring effects.

Then the verse continues: "Others are said to be conventionally existent." Again, "conventionally existent" and conventional truth are synonymous. "Others" here refers to phenomena that are unable to perform functions. These are also called *fictional noneffective phenomena*.

We can see that ultimate truth and functioning phenomena are synonyms, and conventional truth and nonfunctioning phenomena are synonyms. This ties in with the terms we looked at earlier: a *thing* can perform a function and is therefore an ultimate truth, whereas a *nonthing* cannot perform a function and is therefore a conventional truth.

We can further refine what characterizes these two types of phenomena by looking at the next line of the verse: "Those two [types of phenomena are] specifically and generally characterized." Ultimate truths are specifically characterized phenomena, and conventional truths are generally characterized phenomena.

This verse really captures the Sautrantika assertion of an ultimate truth as a real, effective, specifically characterized phenomenon able to perform a function (these terms are all synonyms), and a conventional truth as an unreal, fictional, non-effective, generally characterized phenomenon unable to perform a function (these too are all synonyms).

## Conventional Truth in Sautrantika

Dharmakirti says a generally characterized phenomenon is a concealer truth because the conceptual mind apprehending it obscures the unique entity of the specifically characterized phenomenon. Relative truth, conventional truth, and concealer truth are all translations of the Sanskrit *samvriti satya* (Tib. *kundzob denpa*). Here "concealer truth" seems to give a nicer flavor to Dharmakirti's definition because, although it is conventionally or relatively true, such a phenomenon conceals the ultimate nature of reality from the mind. The ultimate truth of that object is a unique, specifically characterized object, but the mind is obscured from seeing it as it really is because it is *mixed* with the conceptualized image of the object.

Take the two glasses we discussed above. It is virtually impossible for us to apprehend them without any further overlay, whether that overlay is the concept "glass," or "two identical glasses," or "empty glass," or whatever concept we place on top of the actual object. This obscures the object in some way, generalizing a specific.

Conceptual thoughts are selective and eliminative. When we imagine a glass, everything that is *non*-glass is excluded, and what we are left with is a generality. Hence, the complete qualities of the glass cannot be experienced in this way.

The Sautrantika scholars cite certain phenomena that can be fully expressed by language, such as space or selflessness. *Space* is the mere absence of obstruction, nothing more. And because it is neither more nor less than that, language is able to express it. Thus, it is a conventional truth. *Selflessness* is the lack of an intrinsic or inherent self, nothing more; *cessation* is the absence of suffering, nothing more. These can all be fully expressed by language; hence, they are conventional truths. (This is quite different from the view of the Vaibhashikas, where these are seen as ultimate truths.)

How does this fit in with objects in the real world? Let's say I have two books, of different sizes. Even just thinking about them, we can attribute differences to them, but there is also a similarity, their "bookness." This generic or universal image is cited as a conventional truth by this school.

With the glass, the concept of "glass-ness" is mixed with the actual object to obscure the truth. Please don't think this school is saying that concepts are essentially bad; it *is* saying, however, that concepts by their very nature obscure the truth. We couldn't make sense of the world without concepts. Imagine a world without labels. There would be no language, no communication, no transference of knowledge such as this; spiritual attainment would be very difficult. Although maybe, because we would only have direct perceptions, we would already be there! The most important thing a child can learn is language, which will enable her to make generalities about the world around her. As adults, however, we need to see the uses and traps of the conceptual mind—something so few of us do.

Like all the Buddhist philosophical schools, the aim of the Sautrantika school is to show the practitioner ways of developing the mind so that a correct understanding of reality can be reached and difficulties and suffering can be overcome. As one of the two "lower" schools, the final goal of the Sautrantikas is liberation and not enlightenment; consequently, the Sautrantikas speak of the selflessness of person and not the selflessness (or emptiness) of phenomena.[21] Nevertheless, there are many very helpful ideas within the Sautrantika system even for someone bent on full enlightenment.

It is essential that we understand the clear explanation of epistemology and logic in the Sautrantika school if we are to understand the mind. Although we may feel that what they say about ultimate and conventional truth does not go far enough, if we are really honest with ourselves, we have to acknowledge that we haven't yet reached even their level of understanding in the way we live our lives.

In particular, understanding their ideas of ultimate truth—phenomena that are able to perform a function—and conventional truth—phenomena that are unable to perform a function but nevertheless have a parallel to real things—helps us not to jump to immediate judgments and then act upon them precipitously. We are searching for sense pleasures all the time, and our need is so great that it is very easy to confuse the overlay that our desire projects onto an object or event with the actual thing itself. By seeing how much of our "perceived" world is, in fact, imputed by our deluded minds, we can be more skillful about where we put our energies, and concentrate more on "real" things, seeing the danger inherent within unreal expectations and equally unreal memories. Studying Sautrantika views can really help us see the extent of our presumptions and so become more openminded.

In the context of studying tenets, a good grasp of Sautrantika views is especially helpful for understanding the later Madhyamaka views, because many of the arguments leveled by the Madhyamikas address Sautrantika positions specifically. If you understand the Sautrantika position, that will make your grasp of the highest view more profound.

# 5 THE CHITTAMATRA SCHOOL

## The Texts Used in Chittamatra

FROM THE INCEPTION of the Chittamatra school onward, we are very clear about the origin of the various Buddhist schools. We know both the sutras and the commentaries by the great Indian masters that form the core of Chittamatra thought.

As I mentioned in chapter 1, the Mahayana tradition divides all the teachings of the Buddha into three "turnings of the wheel of Dharma." The discourses that constitute the first turning, such as the *Four Noble Truths Sutra*, suggest that phenomena exist from their own side. These scriptures take a very pragmatic approach, focusing on the suffering that we all live with and how to reduce and eliminate it. The Buddha's discourses of the second turning strongly assert that phenomena have no intrinsic nature; as a result, there is a seeming contradiction with the teachings of the first turning. The sutras of the third turning address this contradiction. The specific sutras used by the Chittamatra school are considered to be part of the third turning of the Dharma wheel. The three main sutras they use are the *Buddha Nature Sutra* (*Tathagatagarbha Sutra*), the *Sutra Unraveling the Thought* (*Samdhinirmochana Sutra*) and the *Descent into Lanka Sutra* (*Lankavatara Sutra*).

Of the many commentaries on this school written by the great Indian masters, I will only mention a few of the important ones that wholly or mainly present the Chittamatra system of thought: Maitreya's texts *Ornament of the Great Vehicle Sutras* (*Mahayanasutralamkara*) and *Distinguishing the Middle from the Extremes*, Asanga's *Compendium of Higher Knowledge* (*Abhidharmasamucchaya*) and *Levels of the Mind of Integrated Practice* (*Yogacharyabhumi*), Vasubandhu's *Thirty Stanzas* (*Trimshika*) and *Twenty Verses on Cognition* (*Vimshatika*), Dignaga's *Compendium on Valid Cognition* (*Pramanasamucchaya*), and Dharmakirti's *Ascertainment of Reasoning* (*Pramanavinishchaya*).

There are also texts about this school that were composed by the Tibetan masters, although not as many as those of the Indian masters. Lama Tsongkhapa's *Ocean of Eloquence* is the most important work, but he wrote quite extensively about this school's view in other texts, such as the *Essence of True Eloquence*.

## Chittamatra's Base, Path, and Result

This school has two names. It is called either the *Chittamatra* (Mind Only) school, because the school rejects the existence of reality of objects beyond the mind that knows them, or the *Yogachara* (*Practice of Yoga*) school, because the masters of this school justified their reasoning by referring to the insights they had gained in meditation. (Here, "yoga" [union] refers to meditation as well as to the more physical forms we know today.)

From among the many great Indian masters associated with this school, Asanga is traditionally considered to be its founder. Although the ideas that are unique to the school existed before him, he systematically brought them together and made the philosophy a cohesive one. According to Tibetan tradition, he did not personally hold Chittamatra views, but he most clearly showed the unique features of this school's philosophy.

This school is traditionally divided into *Followers of Scripture* and *Followers of Reason*, the former possibly coming from practitioners who studied Asanga's works and the latter referring to those who studied Dignaga and Vasubandhu. Both the Chittamatra and the next school, the Madhyamaka, are called Mahayana schools, in contrast to the previous two schools. Thus, we will find that this school's assertions of the base, path, and result are very different from those of the two lower schools.

As we have seen, the Vaibhashikas and the Sautrantikas explain that the universe is composed of matter formed by the aggregation of substantial, independent, fundamental atoms of existence, the partless particles, and that these partless particles exist completely independent of the mind observing them. They paint a picture of real objects apprehended by perception, in which the objects are external to and separate from the perceiving consciousness. Object and consciousness are two different entities, and there is a causal relationship between them, the object being the cause of the consciousness and the consciousness being the result.

The Chittamatra school refutes the existence of external objects. That does not mean, however, that it rejects the existence of tables, chairs, houses, and so on. This school rejects the existence of external things that are *independent* of consciousness. The mind exists as an intrinsic truly existing reality, but external objects have no such intrinsic truly existing reality because they exist as objects of our known universe only in relation to the mind observing them.

For the Chittamatrins, external phenomena and the mind perceiving them are not two entirely separate entities; instead, they are two aspects of the same entity. The object arises in dependence on the consciousness apprehending it, and the consciousness apprehending the object arises in dependence on the object. Because they are not two entities but one, there is no causal sequential relationship.

In fact, the Chittamatrin assertions about the base are radically different not only from those of the lower schools but also from the Madhyamaka's. This school is unique in that it asserts that all existent things are divided into three natures, *dependent*, *perfect*, and *imputed*, all three of which are aspects of any single phenomenon. We will look at these more closely below.

Another unique Chittamatrin assertion regards the number of consciousnesses there are. All the other schools place the number of main consciousnesses at six: the five sense consciousnesses and main mental consciousness. This school adds two more: the *mind-basis-of-all* and the *afflictive mental consciousness*, asserting that these minds must exist in order for karma to operate.

As this is a Mahayana school, when presenting the path, Chittamatrins assert two types of selflessness or emptiness: the selflessness of persons and the selflessness of phenomena. The selflessness of persons is almost identical to the assertions of the previous two schools; the selflessness of phenomena, on the other hand, is regarded as a phenomenon's perfect nature, the final mode of existence of an object, which in this school is the nonduality of subject and object.[22]

In addition to the thirty-seven aspects of the path to enlightenment that the two lower schools assert as the practice of the path, the Chittamatra school emphasizes the mind of enlightenment (Skt. *bodhichitta*) and the six perfections (Skt. *paramitas*).

Also, as a Mahayana school, the Chittamatrins present full enlightenment, not just liberation from cyclic existence, as the result of the path. In full enlightenment, the practitioner attains the two bodies of a buddha—the form body (Skt. *rupakaya*) and the truth body (Skt. *dharmakaya*), thus accomplishing the purposes of both self and others. The truth body is often further divided into two: the wisdom truth body (Skt. *jñanakaya*) and the natural truth body (Skt. *svabhavikakaya*); the form body is also further divided into two: the enjoyment body (Skt. *sambhogakaya*) and the emanation body (Skt. *nirmanakaya*).[23] The previous schools do not mention these buddha bodies.


## The Three Natures

Like all the Buddhist philosophical schools, the Chittamatra school attempts to divide all phenomena into reality and what we impute on reality. In doing so, however, the Chittamatrins take a totally different approach from the other schools by asserting that all phenomena have three natures. They are:

1. the dependent nature
2. the imputed nature
3. the perfect nature

If an object is the result of causes and conditions, it therefore has a *dependent* nature, or to use another common name, it is "other-powered." When we apprehend an object, we experience it as if subject (our perception) and object (the perceived object itself) are different entities, distinct and independent. This false distinction of subject and object, say the Chittamatrins, is superimposed onto the object by the mind, so this is its *imputed* nature. Furthermore, we almost always embroider our apprehension of the object in some way, by imputing properties and values onto it that it does not have. These two natures tie us to cyclic existence. Only when we become highly realized can we see that no such subject-object duality actually exists; this nonduality is the *perfect*, or thoroughly established, nature of the object.

## Dependent Nature

Every moment of mind is laden with karmic seeds. Some are ripening, while others are being created by our mental, verbal, or physical actions. Our whole universe is dictated by the creation and ripening of these seeds. The Chittamatra school calls this the *causal flow*, which is the base upon which all else operates.

The dependent nature is what arises in our consciousness from this causal flow due to causes and conditions, and is apprehended as two polarities, the subject (the mind) and the object (the object apprehended by the mind). Although to us it might seem that the eye consciousness is here in our head and the pen is over there—that is, that these are two distinct and very unrelated objects—to the Chittamatrins there is a very strong connection. Our experience of the pen—of the "flow" of the pen—and the pen itself are actually the same entity. There is no difference between these two. The flow of consciousness, from which the subjective and objective aspects arise, is the dependent nature.

Dependent natures include all impermanent phenomena. All the objects of our universe arise, abide, and disintegrate in conjunction with the consciousnesses that apprehend them and are one entity with them.

## Imputed Nature

The apparent distinction between subject and object is a mistaken view that only comes about because of the conceptual, habituated aspect of our mind. The appearance of the mind and its object as two separate, unconnected things is the imputed nature. Subject and object are one entity, but we impute separateness onto them.

Instead of seeing that subject and object both arise from the single flow of experience, we conceptualize different entities—the object grasped by the mind and the mind that grasps the object. "Grasped" and "grasper" are the terms used by the Chittamatra school.

Instinctively, we *assume* that objects exist separate from the mind, but any investigation of objects necessarily involves the mind in some way, so knowledge always has a subjective element. We know there is a pen because we experience the pen. Thus, no object of knowledge exists apart from the mind experiencing it.

Be careful here. It is very easy to look at this idea and then conclude that the object does not exist at all. This is not correct. This school is simply asserting that external objects cannot exist as an object of our universe without taking into account the mind experiencing them. Therefore, although the mind truly exists, the objects of its experience—that is, all the phenomena that comprise our universe—cannot truly exist because they rely on the mind, coming into being as projections of our perception, not as a separate entities.

If the mind is inextricably involved with external objects, then it must also be the case with mental objects, including the all-important concept of "I." Nothing exists within our world that is not an experience of the mind. Object and mind are one entity.

The dependent nature is the mind/object relationship, and the imputed nature is what we put on top of that perception. From the raw experience of the object, we impute the subject/object separation, and then on top of that all the other elements arise: labeling, judging, internal verbalizing, and myriad other conceptual minds. The Chittamatra scholars say that language is what acts most powerfully to construct the imputed nature.

Chittamatrins further divide the imputed nature into two: existent and nonexistent imputed natures. The nonexistent imputed nature is the one we have been looking at: subject and object as different entities, as well as seeing objects as established by their own character, and so on. Nonexistent imputed natures are also things that have no existence at all, conventionally or otherwise, such as the much-loved horns of a rabbit. Existent imputed natures are permanent phenomena—such as unproduced space and abstractions—things that are not products of causes and conditions.


## PERFECT NATURE

Perceiving a duality between the mode of existence of an object and the way the mind conceives the object will not break down until a person has realized a very advanced state of mind. At present, the karmic baggage we carry includes countless lifetimes of conceiving objects as being independently and externally existent; as a result, when an object and a mind perceiving that object arise in the mind, we instinctively see them as two separate things.

As our mind becomes more subtle through meditation, however, that gap between reality and illusion narrows. The veil that the mind throws over an object gets thinner. Let's say we are meditating on our own body. Eventually, when our meditation becomes a complete direct perception free from image generalities, there will be no concepts of body as object and mind as subject. "Body" and "mind meditating on body" will become one. Through meditation the sense of the object being "out there" ceases; the object that we are meditating on becomes like part of the mind itself, and we have thoroughly established the lack of duality between subject and object. Hence, the other name for this nature is *thoroughly established*.

Emptiness for the Chittamatra school is not the absence of essence that other schools ascribe, but the absence of subject-object duality. So what then is the Chittamatra position on the realization of the two kinds of selflessness—of persons and of phenomena? The explanation of the selflessness of persons for Chittamatrins is the same as for the Sautrantikas—there is no self-sufficient person in any way. And the

Chittamatrins agree with the other Mahayana schools that while realizing the selflessness of persons is sufficient for removing the obscurations to liberation, removing the obscurations to omniscience—to buddhahood—requires the realization of the selflessness of phenomena as well. The perfect or thoroughly established nature is often defined in the texts as the aspect of a phenomenon observed in such a way that the observation purifies both obscurations. For the Chittamatrins—unlike the Madhyamikas we will look at below—this means realizing the absence of duality between subject and object. This is the emptiness that a bodhisattva must realize in order to attain full enlightenment.[24]


## The Mind-Basis-of-All

The law of cause and effect, or karma, is a fundamental assertion throughout the whole of Buddhism. No Buddhist disputes that every cause has an effect or that positive actions create positive results and vice versa. At this simple, basic level it is unquestioned. We create the cause; we get the result.

How that happens, however, is a topic about which there is considerable contention. If all phenomena are changing moment by moment—another basic Buddhist tenet—then this moment of mind is different from the previous moment of mind. Consequently, the person I am today is a different entity from the person I was last week or last year, and certainly last lifetime. How can the karma created by that other person ripen on me?

Most Buddhist philosophical schools explain that when an action is completed, a propensity is placed on the consciousness that will ripen later. They assert that the consciousness that stores the propensity must be a neutral one. Just how and where these propensities or seeds are stored is not really clearly addressed, however. Almost all the other schools conclude that the karmic propensities are not form—they certainly aren't physical—nor are they feeling, discrimination, compositional factors, or consciousness itself. So by a process of deduction they conclude that the propensities are stored somewhere within the consciousness.

For the Chittamatrins, however, this seems inadequate, and they have posited a seventh mind, beyond the five sensory consciousnesses and one mental consciousness. They say the six consciousnesses are not really capable of being a mechanism to store the karmic propensities because they fluctuate from positive to negative to neutral and back again. As well, they are temporary and will cease when this life stops. Even during this lifetime, when we become unconscious or when we are in deep meditation, these consciousnesses cease.

When our mind becomes more subtle, the grosser minds are absorbed. When a meditator reaches a very advanced state of meditative absorption, the sensory consciousnesses totally cease. If that is so and the karmic imprints are carried on these consciousnesses, then, the Chittamatra scholars argue, it would be impossible that they could later be reactivated out of nothing. There must be another mind—not these sensory or mental consciousnesses—that does not cease during meditative absorption. It is this seventh mind that carries the seeds that will ripen to reestablish the more normal minds once a meditator comes out of deep meditation.

That mind is the *mind-basis-of-all* (Skt. *alayavijñana*; Tib. *kunzhi namshay*). It functions to act as a base where the karmic seeds are stored. This is a strange-sounding term, but one that is used frequently in Buddhism, and not only in reference to this kind of mind. It is often said that the mind (in general) is the basis for all samsara and nirvana, and in such statements *alaya* or *kunzhi*—"basis-of-all"—is used. Within the Chittamatra teachings, however, it has this very specific meaning.

The Chittamatrins also posit an eighth mind that is not recognized by the other schools, the *afflictive mental consciousness*. This mind filters everything through the sense of a permanent "I." We will examine this later.

## THE FEATURES OF MIND-BASIS-OF-ALL

The mind-basis-of-all is a consciousness; as such, it follows the definition of all consciousnesses in that it is nonmaterial and is clear and knowing. But it is quite different from the other types of consciousness that constitute the totality of our mind, so the Chittamatra scholars have tried to explain its unique qualities to clarify what these differences are. The first way is to look at its features, which are enumerated as four:

1. object
2. aspect
3. nature
4. accompanying minds

For a mind to be "clear and knowing," it must know something. A mind must be a *subject* that takes an *object*. For an eye consciousness, the object is always color and shape, never smell or taste. For a mental consciousness, it is an image or some kind of linguistic construct. The Chittamatra school asserts that everything apprehended by the other minds is also apprehended by the mind-basis-of-all: the five sense objects, such as form, sound, and so on, the five sense consciousnesses, and the mental events that take place within the mind.

The second characteristic of the mind-basis-of-all is its *aspect*, how it apprehends its object. The mind-basis-of-all apprehends but does not actually ascertain its object, so it is called an *inattentive* or *non-ascertaining cognition*.

Whatever comes to this mind is apprehended, in that contact is made, but whereas the other minds fully engage with their objects, the mind-basis-of-all does not actually ascertain its object. It is as if the object brushes over it, leaving nothing but an impression. When we see a desirable object, all the other minds ascertain it, perceiving it and conceptualizing it in various ways, whereas the flavor of that desire stays on the mind-basis-of-all as a propensity.

There are many terms for this—propensity, imprint, seed, latency—but they all mean the same thing. The Tibetan term, *pakchak*, is very nice, *pak* meaning "between" and *chak* meaning "stay," so the whole term literally means "stay between," or, that which stays on between the action and its result. All the other minds ascertain the object but are incapable of retaining anything about it, whereas the sole function of this mind is to retain some sort of taste.

Perhaps the difference between "apprehending" and "ascertaining" is unclear, but it is something that happens in every second of our life. As you read this book, is there a radio playing or are there noises coming from the street? Probably they are loud enough for your ear to hear, so your ear consciousness has apprehended them, but because your focus is on the words on the page, you are not aware of the sounds. They are apprehended but not ascertained. Other consciousnesses can ascertain their object or not—it depends on the amount of attention we pay—but the mind-basis-of-all cognizes but *never* ascertains its object.

The mind-basis-of-all, like all minds, is clear and knowing, but here, "knowing" should not be taken as an overt understanding of the object; it is more in the way of potential. The specific *nature* of the mind-basis-of-all is that it is neutral. Of the three choices—virtuous, nonvirtuous, or neutral—the Chittamatra scholars argue that this mind *must* be neutral; otherwise, as a base for karmic seeds, it would taint them with whatever bias it had. This makes sense, when you think about it. The sole job of the mind-basis-of-all is to store the karmic propensities, which in themselves can be virtuous, nonvirtuous, or neutral. Yet if this mind were nonvirtuous, for example, then no matter what that seed was, it would be flavored by that nonvirtue. The Chittamatrins liken this mind to a pot holding food. If the pot has stored garlic, then there will be some residue of garlic that will get into everything that goes into the pot. Thus, the container must be neutral.

Another important point about the mind-basis-of-all is the number of *accompanying minds* present. If you have read about main minds and mental factors, you will know that apart from whatever main mind is operating—the eye consciousness and so on—there must be other minds, called mental factors, that accompany it.[25] Besides the five *always-present mental factors* that accompany every mind, there are a whole range of others that may or may not be active, such as the object-ascertaining mental factors or the various positive and negative minds.

For any mind to apprehend an object, the five always-present mental factors must be there: contact, discernment, feeling, intention, and attention. The mind-basis-of-all is no exception to this rule. There must be contact, otherwise there is no way that the subject can know its object. In the same way, there must be some degree of discernment (distinguishing one object from another), feeling (even if it is neutral), intention, and attention, although here both attention and intention refer to states of mind that are much more subtle than the English translation would suggest. For instance, intention (Skt. *cetana*; Tib. *semspa*) describes a mind "drawn to" the object in some way, no matter how unconscious that may be.

The mind-basis-of-all follows the rule of all minds in that it is accompanied by these five always-present mental factors; but it is different in that it is never accompanied by any of the others. It does not ascertain its object, so of course the object-ascertaining mental factors do not operate and neither do the other minds—the eleven virtuous mental factors, the root or derivative mental afflictions, and the variable mental factors. This mind must be neutral, as we have seen, so that eliminates all of these mental factors, even the variable ones, which can flick from positive to negative.

## The Properties of Mind-Basis-of-All

For a mind to be the base for the karmic propensities, there are certain properties it must possess. It must be:

1. stable
2. neutral
3. a conditioned compounded phenomenon
4. related to the propensities
5. a basis in its own right

The mind-basis-of-all must be *stable*. Karmic seeds will stay on the mindstream until they ripen, whether that takes a moment or an eon. Therefore, the mind that carries them must be stable, lasting as long as the propensities last, which in effect means until we become enlightened and all karmic seeds have been extinguished. Other minds arise, abide, and cease, but the mind-basis-of-all cannot; otherwise, the propensities it carries will be lost. Therefore, one of the most important qualifications it must have is stability.

Lama Tsongkhapa uses the analogy of the mustard seed. The oil in the seed might not necessarily be stable, but it is stored in the seed for however long the seed is there, to be released when the seed is crushed. If the seed were transient, like the skin of a fruit, it would disintegrate and the oil would be lost.

We have already discussed how the mind-basis-of-all must be *neutral*; otherwise, its bias would affect the seeds it carries. You can see this in everyday life, such as in the case of someone who is very negative doing a good thing. Say a very mean-spirited person sees a hungry beggar and begrudgingly gives the beggar a coin, but then spends the rest of the day regretting his generous action. That positive action is tainted by the overall negative atmosphere in which it was created.

For anyone at all familiar with the most basic Buddhist tenets, being a *conditioned compounded phenomenon* is a logical point. If the mind-basis-of-all were permanent, it would not be able to change or function and, therefore, would not be able to acquire new karmic propensities each time an action is performed. It must be impermanent and hence a compounded phenomenon. Only then will there be a causal interaction between the mind and the action that creates the propensity. Some philosophers use the term *receptive*; the mind-basis-of-all must be receptive to take on karmic seeds, and for that it needs to be a conditioned compounded phenomenon.

The mind-basis-of-all must also be *related to the propensities*. It is not enough that the mind-basis-of-all is a compounded phenomenon. There must be some tie between the action and the mind. A propensity is created in relation to a specific mental or physical action, and it is not as if the propensity from that action simply drops into a big container. It absorbs imprints without partiality, but it is in a dynamic and integrated exchange with the other consciousnesses.

Finally, it must be a *basis in its own right*. If we go back to the example of the mean-spirited person giving a coin to a beggar, it might seem that there is one generous action occurring within a stable base of miserliness. Yet that is not the whole picture. His miserliness was built up year after year—perhaps lifetime after lifetime—through the force of familiarity. That person was not always miserly and certainly won't always be miserly. If that were the case, then there would be no hope for any of us. Habitual tendencies might be strong, but they are not solid or eternal, and they are not a base upon which all other minds arise.

The mind-basis-of-all is a different story. It has not arisen due to the force of familiarity. It has been there as long as there has been mind, and will continue until enlightenment. It is a basis in its own right without relying on other minds to arise. This is the mind that survives at death when all other minds have ceased. In fact, this is why the Chittamatra scholars posited such a mind, to explain what actually takes our karmic propensities from life to life. They say that the mind-basis-of-all will continue until the end of samsara. As long as there is a samsaric mind, this mind endures. One text even states that it will not cease until "nonresidual nirvana and diamond-like samadhi."[26]

## AFFLICTIVE MENTAL CONSCIOUSNESS

The mind-basis-of-all is also a crucial concept for the Chittamatra school when it comes to identifying the sense of self, or "I." For the other schools there are the five aggregates alone, and so the "I" is designated upon one or all of the aggregates. The Chittamatrins reject this, saying that if this were so, then the "I" would not be able to continue from life to life since the aggregates upon which it is designated are absorbed at death. Therefore, the aggregates are not a suitable base for apprehending something as an "I."

For them, however, the mind-basis-of-all qualifies perfectly. Since it holds the karmic propensities and acts as the store for all future experiences, which are based on a sense of "I," then (to them) it is obvious that the "I" abides within the mind-basis-of-all. Because this is a base mind that the other minds are unable to apprehend, the Chittamatrins had to posit an eighth mind, called the *afflictive mental consciousness*. This is what ascribes the sense of self onto whatever action is done (and hence is the cause of all afflictions).

What the Chittamatrins say about the "I" is quite interesting. They assert that although the mind might identify our body or our feeling with the sense of "I," this is, in fact, only temporary. This sense comes and goes and thus cannot stand as a substantial basis for the "I." They say that below all that there runs a continual sense of a permanent, unitary self that underpins and motivates our whole world. Although Buddhism refutes the idea of an eternal self, such as the *atman* in the non-Buddhist Indian schools, this subterranean fundamental driving force that is carried on the mind-basis-of-all comes close to it, although of course it is not a unitary, independent entity. We continue life after life and our karma continues to ripen life after life because the mind-basis-of-all is the mechanism that carries our sense of self. The afflictive mental consciousness is this very sense of "I" that we carry around with us all the time.

The afflicted mental consciousness is also called the *I-maker* (Skt. *ahamkara*), *kara* meaning "to make" and *aham* meaning "I." This is the mind that firmly believes that the "I" really exists, and so this school sees it as the source of all the internal egoistic dialogue.

Like the mind-basis-of-all, the afflictive mental consciousness continues until we become enlightened; but as we progress toward enlightenment, it becomes weaker and weaker. If we exemplify it as a container of seeds, then as we burn off the seeds of unenlightenment, the mind-basis-of-all will still exist as the container, but slowly the afflictive consciousness will get weaker until there are no more seeds left. Then there will also be no more container.

From the Chittamatra perspective, this afflicted mind is the real cause of our problems. It is the white noise of I, I, I that bubbles away all the time. It is the screen that filters everything we experience, the internal discursive conversation that forever runs through our life. This becomes especially clear when we try to meditate. Then we can *really* hear the ego-radio loud and clear.

## How an Object Exists According to Chittamatra

Without further consideration, the name *chitta matra*—mind only—suggests that there is nothing other than mind. As I said above, this is not what the Chittamatra school asserts, and we should not make the mistake of thinking that this school's views are nihilistic. If there is "only mind," does that means all the objects that comprise our world are purely mental constructions? Mind, by definition, is clear and knowing, so does that mean the seat you are sitting on is clear and knowing? Does that mean that Chittamatrins have no friends and no possessions? Of course it is not like that, and in fact the way the Chittamatra school explains how objects exist is very interesting.

The previous two schools assert that when the fundamental building blocks aggregate, they form the objects of the world as we know it; thus, they posit a causal relationship that is not dependent on a mind perceiving it. The Chittamatra school refutes this, asserting that if such an independent external entity were to exist, it would have to possess an intrinsic quality that would project its appearance to consciousness. The existence of an independent external entity furthermore implies that whatever is perceived by a consciousness must be objective—it must actually be there in exactly the way the consciousness perceives it.

According to the Chittamatrins this is not the case. Perception, by definition, is subjective—it is the mind perceiving an object. My perception of an object, such as the page of this book, and your perception will be different, due to our differing flows of consciousness. Perhaps those differences, for culturally similar people, will be slight, but they will be there. Therefore, the page that I perceive does not exist as I perceive it until it is encountered by my consciousness.

Chittamatra philosophers do not refute the existence of objects; they refute their *external* existence. While other philosophies posit an external world that exists in and of itself and the mind as something that responds to it, the Chittamatra school asserts that the mind and its objects arise simultaneously, from the same karmic cause. In every second the whole world as we know it arises and ceases in its apparent duality of subjective and objective aspects, caused by propensities left on the mindstream by our previous actions. They maintain that the duality of subject and object arises only due to the impact of strong imprints from our countless previous lives' association with ignorance. The notion of difference between subject and object is mere hallucination, and this misconception, this grasping at subject and object as separate entities, is the main root of cyclic existence. In fact, the perceiving consciousness and the object it perceives are the same entity.

The concept of "same entity" is difficult to grasp, and there is no clear explanation about it. As we saw in the chapter on the Sautrantika school, the general idea of how an object is apprehended by a sense consciousness is one of cause and effect. There is an external object, which might exist intrinsically (as the lower schools assert) or not (as Madhyamikas assert). In either case, the object is independent of the mind observing it, and it is the cause of the apprehension. A specific example: I see a computer. The computer serves as the *object condition*, which is one of the three causes for my eye consciousness apprehending the computer (the other two being the *empowering condition* and the *preceding condition*, as we have seen). Cause and effect requires sequence, so first there is the computer (the cause), and then there is the eye consciousness perceiving the computer (the effect).

For the Chittamatra school the eye consciousness apprehending the computer and the computer itself arise simultaneously; there is no sequence. We store innumerable imprints on our consciousness, which the Chittamatra scholars call *fundamentally stored*. As such, both the *consciousness* that experiences and the *object* that it relates to arise from these fundamentally stored imprints, and both are of the same substance.

These fundamentally stored karmic imprints are activated by the coming together of various causes and conditions, and when activated the karmic seeds turn into both the object experienced and the consciousness experiencing the object. Thus, object and subject are generated from the same source and have a single substantial cause—that is, they are the same substance.

Imagine I am in a forest on a dark night. I hear a cry and see a dark shape. It is a wolf. I am immediately afraid. From the wolf's side, there is no wolf and no danger. It doesn't think of itself as a wolf or as a terrifying animal. All that is coming from my side. So the entity "wolf" and the danger all arise simultaneously with the mind perceiving it. They are the same substance.

## ULTIMATE TRUTH AND CONVENTIONAL TRUTH ACCORDING TO CHITTAMATRA

For this school's assertions of ultimate truth and conventional truth I will mainly refer to Asanga's *Compendium of Ascertainments* (*Vinishchayasamgrahani*). Other texts from Asanga as well as Maitreya's *Ornament of the Great Vehicle Sutras* also contain detailed explanations of the Chittamatra tenets, particularly those on ultimate truth.

The *Compendium of Ascertainments* states that ultimate truth has five characteristics:[27]

1. inexpressible
2. nondual
3. beyond apprehension by the conceptual mind
4. beyond diversity
5. all of one taste

*Inexpressible*, as the name implies, means that it is impossible to verbally describe ultimate truth precisely. *Nondual* means that within that realization of an arya being in meditative equipoise who is realizing ultimate truth directly, there is no differentiation—no duality—of subject and object. The third characteristic, *beyond apprehension by the conceptual mind*, shows that ultimate truth cannot be realized by ordinary people's cognition but only by the direct perception of an arya being. *Beyond diversity* means that the ultimate truth of an object is not one with its dependent nature, which has many "diversities"—different factors such production, result, causes, conditions, and so on. For example, when we establish the final mode of existence of form, that final mode of existence is the nonduality of subject and object, so all diversities cease.

The final characteristic is that ultimate truths are *all of one taste*. The ultimate truth of a book is the absence of duality of subject and object. Tables, chairs, and so on are different objects, but their ultimate truth is the same. Their final mode of existence is also the mere absence of duality of subject and object. Thus, the ultimate truths of all phenomena are all of one taste.

Of the three natures asserted by the Chittamatrins, perfect nature is an ultimate truth. The other two, dependent nature and imputed nature, are conventional truths. This school asserts that both perfect nature and dependent nature are truly existent, whereas imputed nature is not. Thus, we can see that this school differentiates between things that truly exist—either as ultimate truths (as perfect nature) or conventional truths (as dependent natures)—and things that do not truly exist—imputed natures and fictional conventional truths.

Perfect nature is an ultimate truth because it is the only mode of existence of an object that possesses these five characteristics. It is an ultimate truth because when a practitioner focuses on an object's perfect nature, delusions and ignorance are purified, and continued concentration on the perfect nature leads the practitioner to the complete cessation of suffering. Focusing the mind on the other two natures will not lead to a complete cessation of suffering because they do not have these five characteristics, and in fact, reliance on the imputed and dependent natures leads only to more confusion and suffering.

Dependent nature and perfect nature truly exist because they are facts, they are real. In contrast, the third nature, imputed nature, is fiction, unreal, because it is only conceptually constructed; thus, it does not truly exist. Dependent nature and imputed nature are both conventional truths because their nature is the opposite of perfect nature. When the mind observes them, instead of purifying the mind, it increases the negativities, ignorance, and so forth.

To sum up:

| | | |
|---|---|---|
| ✦ dependent nature | truly existent | conventional truth |
| ✦ imputed nature | conceptually constructed | conventional truth |
| ✦ perfect nature | truly existent | ultimate truth |

In summary then, according to the Chittamatra view, things referred to as external phenomena, such as car, fruit, mountains, and so on, are not separate entities independent of the experience. We can argue that many people apprehend an object in a similar way, but if we examine this closely, we will see that, although we each may use the same language to describe an object, at a subtler level the way we apprehend that object is totally unique to us. My perception of a Picasso painting (or even of an apple) will be different from yours, even if we both love it.

How do I know that the table in my living room exists? I can see it, I can feel it, I can use all my sense faculties to experience the table. But why do I then label it "table"? Why not "that pile of wood over there"? Because its legs and top are constructed in such a way that I can use it as a table. I know it by its function; it is used to hold up my books, my glass of water, my computer. For me "table" is a concept—something I use to eat at, to read at, to work at.

Does this table—the concept of table, the thing that functions in this way—exist outside my consciousness? Naturally, the four bits of wood are there, and the flat surface on top, but does the object "table" exist without my mind giving it the label?

The Chittamatra school would say no. The only way I can prove something exists is by my perception; therefore, the thing cannot exist apart from my perception. The table exists because my eye consciousness sees. On that base we build the entire "conceptualized aspect" as a table.

This is quite difficult to accept, if we come at it with our standard logic. In fact, if you investigate, it is very interesting. The Chittamatrins are not rejecting the table. They assert that the object we label "table" exists, but that to prove the table exists requires consciousness. There is no other way except through seeing, hearing, smelling, touching, and so on. This is something really worth investigating.

Only the mind can prove the existence of something. That does not mean the thing is just in our mind. But things only exist when consciousness apprehends them. That we see consciousness and object as separate is, in the Chittamatra view, the starting point of all our mistakes.

# 6 THE MADHYAMAKA SCHOOL

## The Major Texts and Teachers of the Madhyamaka School

THE FOURTH AND LAST—and most important in our tradition—of the philosophical schools studied in Tibetan Buddhism is the Madhyamaka (Middle Way) school, so called because all its presentations emphasize the middle way that is free from the extremes of nihilism and eternalism.

This school takes its view from all the Mahayana sutras, especially the *Perfection of Wisdom* (*prajñaparamita*) sutras. There are extensive, medium-length, and short *Perfection of Wisdom* sutras, the most famous one being the *Heart of Wisdom Sutra*, or *Heart Sutra*. We find almost identical versions of the *Heart Sutra* in many different languages throughout all the Mahayana traditions, with only slight differences in the introductions.

In the *Compendium of Sutras* (*Sutrasamucchaya*), a central work among his many treatises, Nagarjuna collected many quotations from the sutras for the purpose of presenting the Madhyamaka view; thus, this text is considered to be a root source of Nagarjuna's views on emptiness. Another seminal work of Nagarjuna is his *Fundamental Treatise on the Middle Way* (*Mulamadhyamakakarika*).

There are many key texts that present the Madhyamaka view. I will list some so you will know them when you come across them as you read about emptiness and the two truths. Nagarjuna's close disciple, Aryadeva, wrote important works such as *Four Hundred Stanzas* (*Chatuhshataka*). Other important works are Buddhapalita's *Commentary on "Fundamental Wisdom"* (*Mulamadhyamaka-vritti*), as well as Bhavaviveka's *Blaze of Reasoning* (*Tarkajvala*) and his *Lamp of Wisdom* (*Prajnapradipa*). Chandrakirti wrote *Clear Words* (*Prasannapada*), which is also a commentary on Nagarjuna, as well as *Commentary on the "Four Hundred Stanzas"* (*Chatuhshataka-tika*) and *Supplement to the Middle Way* (*Madhyamakavatara*) together with its autocommentary.

Other texts include Jñanagarbha's *Differentiation of the Two Truths* (*Satyadvayavibhanga*) and its autocommentary; Shantarakshita's *Ornament of the Middle Way* (*Madhyamakalamkara*) and its autocommentary; and Kamalashila's *Stages of Meditation* (*Bhavanakrama*).

In addition, there are many commentaries written by Tibetan masters. As you can see, the Madhyamaka school has a huge textual base. From the earliest works of Nagarjuna up to those composed in the eleventh century by Kamalashila and Shantarakshita, all are still studied in Tibetan monasteries today, and although some date back almost two thousand years, all are as vital as when they were written.

His Holiness the Dalai Lama quite often says that Tibetan Buddhism's tradition stretches right back to the incredible Indian monastic universities, especially Nalanda, so it is imperative to keep the tradition that comes from Nagarjuna alive, to some extent through the great scholastic tradition still active in the Tibetan monasteries, but even more through the many practitioners who actually seek to realize what these great masters taught.

## The Two Subschools

Nagarjuna and Aryadeva are known as the fathers of the Madhya-maka school. Because all the later masters treat their works as the pri-mary texts that present the source of Madhyamaka thought (despite some slight differences), the first Tibetan scholars named Nagarjuna and Aryadeva the "fundamental Madhyamikas" and the later Indian masters the "supporter Madhyamikas."

Nagarjuna and Aryadeva were followed by Buddhapalita and Bhavaviveka, who differed in their interpretations of what their pred-ecessors had meant. There were some key points in Madhyamaka phi-losophy that had not yet been explicitly explained, so when Buddhapalita wrote his commentary on Nagarjuna's *Fundamental Treatise on the Middle Way*, he presented the view that Nagarjuna asserted the existence of the external world but that things did not have intrinsic nature. Buddhapalita also asserted that Nagarjuna had used consequential arguments instead of syllogisms alone to prove points, syllogisms—sheer logic—not being powerful enough to culti-vate the inferential cognizer needed to understand ultimate truth. Consequential arguments are debates wherein ideas are challenged until they collapse into absurdity.

When Bhavaviveka saw Buddhapalita's commentary, he strongly disagreed with these points in both his *Blaze of Reasoning* and *Lamp of Wisdom*. From then on these great masters' different understandings formed two distinct strains of thought within the Madhyamaka school. Bhavaviveka is considered to be the founder of the Svatantrika Madhyamaka (Middle Way Autonomy) subschool.

Still later, Chandrakirti, in both his *Clear Words* and his *Commen-tary on the "Four Hundred Stanzas,"* refuted Bhavaviveka's views and asserted that Buddhapalita had interpreted Nagarjuna correctly. Chandrakirti is therefore considered to be the founder of the

Prasangika Madhyamaka (Middle Way Consequence) subschool. In this way the Madhyamaka school, at least from the perspective of the later Tibetan masters, is divided into two distinct subschools.

Unlike Chandrakirti and Buddhapalita who both assert the existence of external objects in general, there are some Madhyamaka masters, such as Shantarakshita and his disciple Kamalashila, who deny that external objects exist.

Through the great kindness of Shantarakshita, Kamalashila, and Atisha, Buddhism developed in Tibet. At first Bhavaviveka's system was dominant, but later on the Prasangika Madhyamaka view became the stronger and more widely spread. If you look at the present situation of the four traditions within Tibetan Buddhism—Nyingma, Sakya, Kagyu, and Gelug—all four profess their view to be that of the Prasangika Madhyamaka. As well, within all the traditions there are extensive commentaries on the Indian masters, all presented from the Prasangika perspective. Therefore, almost all Tibetan practitioners regard the Prasangika Madhyamaka view as the most profound presentation on the reality of things and events.

## The Importance of the Two Truths for Madhyamaka

We have examined the assertions of the earlier Buddhist philosophical schools about the base, in which different categories were used to ascertain what comprise existent phenomena: conditioned and unconditioned phenomena, generally and specifically characterized phenomena, contaminated and uncontaminated phenomena, and so on. The Madhyamaka school is no different from the other schools in its need to categorize existent phenomena. The Madhyamaka assertions pertaining to the base rest on the all-important division of the two truths, where existent things (called "objects of knowledge" by them) are asserted to be either conventional truths or ultimate truths.

The explanation of the base as the two truths is traced back to the teachings of the Buddha, such as those in the *Meeting of the Father and Son Sutra* (*Pitaputrasamagama Sutra*):

> Thus it is: The Tathagata understands both conventional and ultimate.
> Objects of knowledge are exhausted within these two:
> Concealer truths and ultimate truths.[28]

This sutra clearly explains that what we need to realize about the base of existent things is the two truths: concealer (relative or conventional) truth and ultimate truth. Most Madhyamaka texts rely on this quotation to show how vital these two concepts are. A similar thought is expressed in Nagarjuna's *Fundamental Treatise on the Middle Way*:

> The teachings of the Buddha
> Depend entirely on the two truths.
> [There are either] worldly concealer truths
> Or ultimate truths.
>
> Whoever fails to understand the difference
> Between these two truths
> Fails to understand the nature
> Of the Buddha's profound doctrine.[29]

From this and many similar statements, it is clear that, for Madhyamikas, an understanding of the two truths is not only important in order to understand the base, but essential if we are to follow the path and achieve the result of enlightenment.

An unmistaken path can only come from a clear understanding of the two truths. Understanding conventional truth enables the practitioner to develop the method side—compassion, concentration, and ethics—whereas understanding ultimate truth leads to the realization of the wisdom side—emptiness. These realizations will, in turn, result in the two buddha bodies, the truth body and the form body. Quite simply, we are in an unenlightened state purely through ignorance of the two truths, and conversely, we can only make progress and eventually attain the result of full enlightenment by realizing them.

This school's entire presentation focuses on developing both method and wisdom on the path to enlightenment. The sixteen aspects of the four noble truths and the bodhisattva activities of the six perfections are all presented by way of the base—that is, the two truths.

The ninth chapter of *A Guide to the Bodhisattva's Way of Life* (*Bodhicharyavatara*), where Shantideva explains emptiness, opens with:

> All of these practices were taught
> By the Mighty One for the sake of wisdom.
> Therefore, those who wish to pacify suffering
> Should generate this wisdom.

> Deceptive truths and ultimate truths
> Are accepted as the two truths.[30]

The diversity of the Buddha's teachings is due to the multiplicity of sentient beings' mental dispositions, yet all are designed to lead to the wisdom that understands the ultimate reality contained within the knowledge of the two truths. People who want to be free from suffering need to cultivate an understanding of reality, the wisdom of ultimate truth, while developing the method side of the practice, which entails a thorough understanding of conventional truth. There is no other way.

Many similar statements by masters from Nagarjuna right up to contemporary teachers emphasize the importance of the two truths. For example, His Holiness the Dalai Lama often says that we need to understand the teachings on the two truths to comprehensively understand the Buddhadharma.[31]

## Conventional Truth in Madhyamaka

### THE MEANING OF SAMVRITI SATYA

As I have said, the Sanskrit term for the first of the two truths is *samvriti satya*. The etymology of the term *samvriti* is interesting. *Sam* is either an abbreviation of *samyak*, which means "reality," or of *samanta*, which means "entirely," and *vrt* means "to obstruct," so taken together scholars have read this to be "that which entirely conceals reality." This corresponds to the Tibetan term *kundzob*, which literally means "all covered."

In his *Illumination of the Thought*, Lama Tsongkhapa defines conventional truth as:

> ...a phenomenon found by a conventional valid cognizer apprehending a false object of knowledge.[32]

In Chandrakirti's *Supplement to the Middle Way*, his commentary on Nagarjuna's *Fundamental Treatise on the Middle Way*, is the following verse:

> Ignorance conceals nature; therefore, it is conventional.
> What is created by this ignorance appears to be true.

So the Buddha spoke of this as a conventional truth,
and thus, manufactured things exist only conventionally.[33]

Here we can see that because ignorance conceals reality it is called
*conventional*. All "manufactured things"—those things that come into
existence due to causes and conditions—are seen by the true-grasping,
ignorant mind as having a true—i.e., causeless and independent—
nature that they don't have; therefore, that mind conceals their actual
mode of existence. By superimposing a sense of true existence onto
the object, the reality of the object is obscured. Because of this, it is a
*concealer* truth, true for the ignorant true-grasping mind, but concealing the ultimate truth of the object.

It is important to understand that to the ignorant mind it is true,
which is why it is called a concealer or conventional *truth*. Things and
events such as form, sound, body, and tables are *grasped* by the true-
grasping mind as if they have a true nature, and they also *appear* to
that mind as if they have a true nature. There is concordance between
the way the mind grasps the object and the way the object appears to
the mind. Within that context it is called a conventional or concealer
truth.

Like many words, the term *samvriti* changes meaning depending on
the context, so it is good to be clear of the exact meaning in whatever
text we are reading. In the *Descent into Lanka Sutra* it says:

[Although] things are produced conventionally,
Ultimately they have no nature.
Whatever is mistaken about this lack of nature
Is said to be conventional with regard to reality.[34]

In this verse the word *samvriti*—translated here as "conventional"—is used twice. The first use refers to all existent phenomena,

which exist conventionally, including ultimate truth. The "conventional" in the last line refers to the mind that is ignorant, in that it is mistaken with regard to the ultimate nature of things and events. This refers to the ignorant true-grasping mind. "The lack of nature" here means the lack of true existence. Things and events lack true existence, but the ignorant mind superimposes this true nature on top of their actual existence. "With regard to reality" shows that the conventional mind obscures the real nature of things. The first use of *samvriti* refers to all things and events whereas the second use refers to the particular state of mind that overlays true existence on the actual nature of things and events.

In general, there are three main possibilities for the Sanskrit term *samvriti*:

1. an ignorant consciousness that conceals reality
2. that which is interdependent
3. worldly conventions

In his *Ocean of Reasoning*, Lama Tsongkhapa expands on this:

"Convention" refers to lack of understanding, or ignorance; that is, that which obscures or conceals the way things really are. This is explained in this way as the Sanskrit term for "convention," *samvriti*, can mean *concealment* as well. But not *all* conventions are said to be concealers.

Alternatively, "convention" can be taken to mean *mutually dependent*. Since things must be mutually dependent, the meaning of "untrue" is that they do not essentially have the ability to stand on their own. This approach to explaining the meaning of the word is applicable to "ultimate truth" as well; but the word "conventional" is not used to refer to it. This is like, for example, the word "grown-from-the-lake" [*tsokyey*] which is literally applicable to a frog but is not used to refer to a frog, but to a lotus.

Alternatively, "convention" can be taken to mean *signifier*, that is, mundane nominal convention. Convention in this sense is also said to be characterized by expressions and the objects of expressions, awareness and objects of awareness, etc. Therefore, "subjective convention" does not refer merely to expressions or to awareness.[35]

It is clear that "conventional" in the expression *conventional truth* sometimes refers to the ignorant mind that grasps on to things and events as if they exist truly (meaning 1). However, whatever appears to that ignorant mind is not necessarily conventional truth. For the self-grasping mind things appear as truly existent, but "truly existent" is not a synonym for conventional truth. The difference will be spelled out more clearly in the next section on valid and invalid cognition.

"Conventional" can also refer to all dependent phenomena (meaning 2), whether conventional truths or ultimate truths. This is what the text is referring to with the mention of that which is "grown from a lake." Taken literally this could be either a frog or a lotus, but for ancient culture this was an idiom for lotus. The analogy is that, both conventional objects and ultimate truths have conventional existence (they are dependent phenomena) but ultimate truth is not a conventional truth (it is not an object of a concealing mind).

For the Vaibhashika school, a conventional truth is that which is interdependent, i.e., the second interpretation of "conventional." Things are interdependently true or "real." In other contexts, whatever is agreed upon as a truth by worldly conventions is a relative or conventional truth, the third interpretation. This includes all our worldly knowledge, such as the fact that water flows downhill and that a day is a twenty-four-hour cycle of day and night.

For both Madhyamaka subschools, however, *conventional truth* refers to an ignorance that conceals reality, the first meaning. This is the particular ignorance that covers everything, that deceives us about our entire existence. My teacher exemplified this as a two-faced friend, the sort of person who is charismatic and outwardly genuine but who does everything for ulterior motives. He entertains and flatters us, and it takes a long time to realize he is only doing this to use us in some way.

A relative or conventional truth is a *truth* because it *works* conventionally. I see a book, and my mind registers "book." There is concurrence between the consciousness and the object of the consciousness. We are deceived, however, in that the object appears to us to be inherently existent, whereas it is not. Of course, logically we can understand its interdependence; we can understand that it is a dependent arising that depends on its parts, or that it is changing moment by moment. Logically we can accept that it has no intrinsic existence. But that is not how the object appears to us. The world we know through conventional truths appears to give some degree of comfort and stability, but in reality it brings us difficulties.

## The Accuracy of Direct Valid Cognizers

Both Svatantrika and Prasangika proponents agree on the definition of conventional truth, but they diverge in their explanations of the level of subtlety that constitutes a conventional truth. For Svatantrikas, an object cognized by direct perception is an unmistaken conventional truth. Not so for Prasangikas.

Consciousness can be divided into two, valid and invalid. With regard to valid cognition (Skt. *pramana*; Tib. *tsema*) both subschools assert that there are two types of valid cognizers: *direct* perceivers (or direct valid cognizers) and *inferential* valid cognizers.

The Svatantrika masters, such as Bhavaviveka and Kamalashila, assert that direct valid cognizers, such as an eye consciousness directly apprehending an object, are free from any mistaken element at all. There can be wrong direct perceivers, such as when we see two moons by squinting, but apart from those direct perceivers that are disturbed by immediate causes and conditions, all other direct perceivers are valid and unmistaken.

Prasangika scholars disagree, asserting that in unenlightened beings, no matter how valid or accurate the perceptions are with respect to their object, they are affected by the long-term appearance of the inherent nature of things and events. The only exception to this is the direct perception of emptiness by a being in meditative equipoise.

This is a huge and vital difference between the two subschools. Masters like Bhavaviveka assert that although every thing and event is empty of true existence, it still has its own established nature, an inherent or intrinsic nature. The distinction between *truly existing* and *inherently existing* is a very subtle one, and something we will explore in the fifth book of the *Foundation of Buddhist Thought* series, *Emptiness*. Basically, the Svatantrika line is that a phenomenon does not exist truly in that it relies on causes and conditions to come into existence, and yet there is still some quality about it that is unique and inherent. We incorrectly see a chair as being causeless—a truly existing chair—whereas it is no more than the basis of designation which we label "chair." Nonetheless, there is an inherent base and an inherent label. Prasangikas completely deny this, saying even this degree of inherent existence is false.

For the Svatantrikas, my eye consciousness perceiving a book is unmistaken in every sense. The book has its own established inherent nature; my eye consciousness perceives it as having that established inherent nature, and so it is unmistaken, quite simply because that is how things and events exist.

From the point of view of Prasangika masters such as Chandrakirti, not only are things and events lacking true existence, but they also have no established inherent nature from their own side whatsoever. Thus, perceiving such an inherent nature in objects is the mistake in direct valid cognizers. An object appears not only to conceptual consciousnesses but also to direct perceivers as having a true and inherent nature. No matter how valid a direct cognizer may be, there is still the mistaken element of the object appearing as if it has inherent existence. My eye consciousness perceiving a book is valid and correct, but within that process there is an element wherein the book appears to my eye consciousness as having a true and inherent book nature. In that it is mistaken.

## How Inferences Realize an Object

The two subschools differ in their ideas on valid cognition in other ways. All Buddhist schools assert three types of direct perceivers—sense, mental, and yogic direct perceivers.[36] Some Svatantrika masters, like Dharmagarbha, also assert a fourth type, the self-knowing direct perceiver.

This is very similar to the assertion by the Chittamatra school that when a consciousness meets an object there are two aspects to that consciousness, the *objective* aspect that apprehends the object itself, and the *subjective* aspect that is aware of itself apprehending the object. As with the Chittamatra school, this second aspect is called a *self-knowing direct perceiver*, and is part of any direct valid cognizer. Prasangika masters and even some Svatantrika masters refute this.

The main difference between the two subschools' explanations of valid cognition, however, regards how an inferential valid cognizer realizes its object. Whereas conceptual consciousnesses in general are faulty, an inference that has attained a clarity and certainty about an object can in fact realize its object without fault. This is called an *inferential valid cognizer*. Without first going through this stage of valid inference, it is impossible to realize emptiness directly. We must first go through concepts before we can go beyond them in direct realization.

Masters from both subschools assert that many hidden objects can only be understood through inferential cognizers, specifically those subtle modes of existence of things and events such as impermanence and emptiness. Ordinary people cannot cognize these hidden objects directly, only inferentially. The difference here between the subschools is not in how they view the consciousness itself, but in the methodology used to gain such an inference. Svatantrika masters like Bhavaviveka assert that in order to have an inferential valid cognizer, say of emptiness, we need to use an *autonomous sign*, a kind of self-existent reason. This is, in fact, the vital thrust of the *Svatantrika* approach and why they are called the Svatantrika Madhyamaka— Middle Way Autonomy—school. For the Svatantrikas, the initial realization of emptiness through an inferential cognizer can only take place by means of such an autonomous sign.

Their whole method of making an assertion is to use syllogisms in three parts: the *subject*, which is the subject under discussion, the *predicate*, which is the argument raised about the subject, and the *sign*, or reason. Such syllogisms are said to stand on their own as proof of an argument. In order for the reason to be reached and the assertion made, the thesis must be established from its own side. And so, when these masters formulate the syllogism to prove the thesis that all things and events are empty of true existence, that thesis must be established from its own side, by way of its own power, as an "autonomous" sign.

In a Buddhist syllogism there are three modes: the property of the position, the forward pervasion, and the counter pervasion.[37] When the syllogism is proposed between two parties in a debate, it must have all these modes in order for it to be a valid statement. If any one mode is missing, the syllogism is not valid. To the Svatantrikas, verifying the validity of the three modes is what establishes something by its own power.

By contrast, Prasangika masters like Chandrakirti say that in order to have a valid inferential cognizer of a hidden object such as emptiness, we do not need any form of autonomous syllogism established from its own side. Instead, it is enough to make use of consequential statements, which are statements that reject wrong conceptions. As with Svatantrika, this mode of enquiry gives this subschool its name, the *Prasangika* Madhyamaka—Middle Way Consequence—school. For example, to refute the Chittamatra assertion of true existence or the Svatantrika assertion of inherent existence, the Prasangikas take those assertions to their logical limits so that their absurdities are uncovered, which is enough to bring about valid inferential cognizers that realize the absence of true existence and the absence of inherent existence.

Moreover, the Prasangikas say, as soon as you believe an autonomous sign, then what you are asserting is that something exists from its own side, that there is some kind of inherent entity. This is a mistake, say the Prasangikas. Any methodology that seeks to generate a valid inferential cognizer realizing emptiness based on something that is seen to exist from its own side is flawed. The only valid method, therefore, is simply to systematically reject whatever misconceptions other assertions raise about the object under analysis. That process in itself, Prasangika scholars assert, will bring about valid inferential cognizers.

## THE EXISTENCE OF EXTERNAL OBJECTS

Some Svatantrika Madhyamaka masters propound realist notions from the two lower philosophical schools, specifically that external phenomena come into existence due to the aggregation of partless particles. Other Svatantrika masters refute that kind of existence and follow the Chittamatra school closely, rejecting the existence of external things. Therefore, the Svatantrika Madhyamaka school is further subdivided into two: the *Sautrantika Svatantrika*, whose main master was Jñanagarbha, and the *Yogachara Svatantrika*, whose main master was Shantarakshita.

Prasangika Madhyamaka masters like Chandrakirti also say that external objects exist. Even though they use same the term as the lower schools, the Prasangikas' assertion of how external objects exist is quite different. They do not assert that external objects exist through the aggregation of partless particles. For the Prasangika masters, external objects exist simply because they are perceived by a conventional valid cognition that is not investigating their ultimate nature. Without any investigation, we normal people see books or chairs, and to us they exist. Therefore, say the Prasangikas, on a conventional level, external objects exist. This is noted by Lama Tsongkhapa in his *Great Treatise on the Stages of the Path* (*Lamrim Chenmo*):

> Therefore, although the masters Chandrakirti and Bhavaviveka both accept that external objects exist, they seem to differ in how they assert sensory consciousnesses and their objects.[38]

## REAL AND UNREAL CONVENTIONAL TRUTHS

A strong clue to the distinction between the two subschools comes with the Svatantrika explanation of real and unreal conventional truths.

Svatantrika Madhyamaka masters assert that conventional truths can be divided into two categories, real and unreal. Tables, chairs, books, persons, and so forth are real conventional truths in that worldly beings take them as true because that is how they appear to their consciousnesses. Unreal conventional truths are things for which a disparity exists between how those objects are and how they appear, even on this conventional level. The reflection of a face in a mirror, an echo, an illusion created by a magician, and so forth are unreal because even a worldly consciousness can understand the discrepancy. In other words, the Svatantrika Madhyamaka masters are categorizing different levels of conventional truths, one that is apparently real to worldly consciousnesses and one that is not.

In contrast, Prasangika Madhyamaka proponents make no such division. For them *all* conventional truths are unreal in that they are all falsities. There is no actual "truth" in the nature of conventional truth. For them the face and the reflection of the face in the mirror are both deceptive because they both appear to be inherently existent. Therefore, both are "unreal." However, the Prasangikas are not saying that there is no difference in the mode of existence between the face and the reflection. The face is true, right, and real from the perspective of the mundane world. On the other hand, the reflection of the face that appears as a real face is false, wrong, and unreal from the perspective of the mundane world. Here, it's important to understand that we are talking about conventionalities—the world seen from our usual mundane perspective—and that this is not related in any way to the distinctions between "truly existing" and "inherently existing" that Prasangikas make when discussing ultimate truths.

For Prasangikas, to apprehend something as a truth is to apprehend it as it actually exists. There must be full concordance between its mode of appearance and its mode of existence. Conventional truths are also called concealer truths for the very reason that they are faulty, because they all—whether we are speaking of a real face or a reflection—appear to be inherently existent, whereas none exist in that way.

Here again it comes back to levels of subtlety of understanding the final mode of existence of things and events. Bhavaviveka strongly rejects the Chittamatra concepts of dependent and perfect natures as being true natures. He refutes the notion that things and events exist *truly*, but still asserts that on a worldly conventional level there is no mistake when a consciousness perceives an object as existing *inherently*. For Chandrakirti, on the other hand, there is no difference between "truly existing" and "inherently existing" and both must be refuted.

## Ultimate Truth in Madhyamaka

### EMPTINESS

Both Madhyamaka subschools assert that ultimate truth is the final mode of existence of things and events. For the Svatantrika Madhyamaka subschool, that means the absence of true existence; that is their emptiness. Like the Prasangikas, they assert two types of emptiness, of person and of phenomena, but unlike the Prasangikas, they do not assert that the emptiness of phenomena is synonymous with the complete cessation of suffering, the third noble truth. For the Prasangikas, emptiness and cessation are the same.

Svatantrika texts tend to stay with the term *selflessness*, and so for them the path that leads to enlightenment is through an understanding of these two selflessnesses, of person and of phenomena. The selfless-ness of phenomena for them is the absence of true existence of phe-nomena, whereas the selflessness of person refers to the unfindability of a self among the five aggregates,[39] the same selflessness that is pre-sented in the lower schools.

For the Svatantrika Madhyamaka, hearers (Skt. *shravaka*) and soli-tary realizers (Skt. *pratyekabuddha*) must realize only the emptiness of *true* existence to achieve liberation (Skt. *nirvana*) and become an arhat, whereas for the Prasangika Madhyamaka, to achieve liberation these arhats must have a direct realization of emptiness, which means not just realizing the absence of *true* existence—the absence of cause-less, concrete object within the inherent base and label—but of *inher-ent* existence as well—the fact that there is no inherent nature within even the base and label. Without realizing the emptiness of both per-sons and phenomena, there is no way to achieve liberation and, of course, no way to achieve full enlightenment.

## The Meaning of Paramarta Satya

While there is general agreement within both subschools that ulti-mate truth is the final mode of existence of things and events, they differ when it comes to actually explaining the term *ultimate truth*.

In Sanskrit the term for ultimate truth is *paramarta satya*, and in Tibetan it is *dondam denpa*. It is worth looking at the Tibetan ety-mology to see the difference of interpretation. For the Svatantrika Madhyamaka, *don*, the first syllable, refers to the final mode of exis-tence of the object, and *dam*, the second syllable, refers to the supreme mind apprehending that final mode of existence, which is an arya being's mind in meditative equipoise.[40] So *dondam* is the *supreme* mind ascertaining the *fact*, the final mode of existence. In other words, "ultimate" is here broken into two levels, the objective, the supreme fact of the mode of existence (*don*), and the subjective, the mind apprehending it (*dam*).

*Denpa* means "truth" in that there is no deception. An arya being's mind in meditative equipoise realizes things and events exactly as they exist.

But when Prasangika Madhyamaka scholars explain the term *dondam* they do not break it into two syllables treated separately (one object, one subject) as in the Svatantrika explanation. Here, *dondam* is the "supreme fact"—that the final mode of existence of an object is its lack of true and inherent existence. The Prasangikas, therefore, interpret ultimate truth from the objective side, not the subjective. Also, as in the Svatantrika explanation, *denpa* here means "truth"; there is no deception in the ultimate mode of existence.

Chandrakirti, in his *Clear Words*, says:

> Since it is a fact [*don*] and it is supreme [*dam pa*] as well, it is ultimate [*don dam*]. And since *it* is true, it is the ultimate truth.[41]

In his *Ocean of Reasoning*, Lama Tsongkhapa explains this:

> Therefore, Chandrakirti does not maintain, as do others, that the uncontaminated wisdom of meditative equipoise is the supreme and that the ultimate is its object. He instead maintains that "ultimate truth" indicates both that [it] is a fact and that it is supreme. The respect in which ultimate truth is a truth is that it is nondeceptive.[42]

## ULTIMATE MIND

What distinguishes conventional and ultimate truths is not the object but the way the object is ascertained by the mind. Analyzed by a conventional mind, the object is a conventional truth; analyzed by an ultimate mind, which sees the lack of inherent existence of the object, it is an ultimate truth. It's not that emptiness is tacked on to the object as something separate. The object is the same. The difference is epistemological rather than ontological. Chandrakirti's *Supplement to the Middle Way* says:

> The Buddha says that all things have two aspects,
> And they may be perceived correctly or falsely.
> What is perceived correctly is ultimate truth,
> And what is perceived falsely is conventional truth.[43]

Within every existent thing or event are two aspects, the aspect found by "perceivers of reality" and the aspect found by "perceivers of falsities." *All* things and events—important and unimportant, enlightened and unenlightened—have these two aspects.

A perceiver of reality is also called an "ultimate mind," that is, the consciousness analyzing the final mode of existence of an object. The aspect found by such a mind is called an ultimate truth, or emptiness, or *thusness*. The aspect of an object found by a perceiver of falsities—a conventional mind—is called a conventional or concealer truth.

It is not that there are two modes of existence of consciousness, each perceiving the object differently, one consciousness existing conventionally and one ultimately. Here, we are referring to the mind's mode of enquiry, not its mode of existence.

One avenue for investigating ultimate and conventional truths is by looking at things in terms of subject, object, and action. For instance, if we analyze me writing this book, then the writer, the book, and the activity of writing can be analyzed from these two angles. I can use many criteria in exploring this subject/object/action relationship, and all of these will be conventional minds analyzing conventional truths *except* the mind that seeks the final mode of existence of the writer, the book, and the writing. Whether we are simply observing that there is a book, or a writer; whether we are judging the worth of both; whether we are exploring how subject, action, and object interrelate; or whether we are analyzing the impermanence of each of the three—*all* these kinds of examination are engaged in by conventional valid cognizers analyzing conventional truths. They are conventional truths because they are true to the mundane, conventional mind, and they are conventional valid cognizers because they do not ascertain the way the objects actually exist. Book, writer, and writing all still appear to the consciousness as having intrinsic reality, whereas in reality they do not. Consequently, they are called false objects of knowledge and concealer truths.

On the other hand, when an ultimate mind analyzes the final mode of existence of the writer, the book, or the activity of writing by seeing the lack of intrinsic existence, there is no disparity between the way the object exists and how it appears to that mind. Although this is an instance of an ultimate valid cognizer using ultimate analysis to apprehend an ultimate truth, that *does not mean*, however, that the mind itself exists ultimately. Nothing exists ultimately.

According to the Gelug tradition, there are actually two stages of ultimate mind—the *analytical stage*, wherein the conceptual mind analyzes the ultimate mode of existence of things and events, and the *nonconceptual stage*, where the mind moves beyond the conceptual to realize the wisdom of emptiness directly.

Both minds realize the same object—an emptiness of inherent existence—but the quality of the mind is different. The process must start with analysis, by means of which we slowly develop an inferential realization that things have no inherent or intrinsic existence. Eventually, our analytical mind settles down and can be placed single-pointedly on that absence in a state that we call *meditative equipoise*, where the mind does not waver at all from its object. There is no more analyzing because our mind resides firmly in the awareness of emptiness. This is the direct realization of emptiness, where there is no awareness of an "I" who is thinking "emptiness," but only emptiness itself.

## Ultimate Existence

According to the Madhyamikas, ultimate truth exists but ultimately existent objects do not. Although this might seem at first glance to be confusing, the confusion is in the closeness of terms rather than concepts. An ultimate truth is the emptiness of a phenomenon, the fact that it is empty of existing independently. To *exist* ultimately, on the other hand, means exactly that, to exist independently of other things and events, something that is impossible according to the Madhyamaka. The two terms actually look at the same thing from opposite angles, one examining how an object really exists, and the other, how it doesn't.

It is traditionally taught that to exist ultimately an object would have to fulfill two criteria: an object would have to (1) be able to withstand analysis by an ultimate mind, and (2) exist objectively without needing to be ascertained by a nondefective awareness.

These are logical criteria used in debate and are, therefore, expressed in very precise language. However, if we pick them apart, they are not too difficult to understand. We have just determined what an ultimate mind is. Something that can withstand analysis by an ultimate mind is something that will be findable by such analysis. The Madhyamaka philosophers argue that there is no such phenomenon.

If an ultimate mind is that which analyzes the final mode of existence of an object, then that final mode must be findable. This is the core of the meditations on emptiness. When analyzing an object we explore whether there is any aspect of the object that exists in and of itself. By determining the unfindability of the object from its own side, we use the ultimate mind to come to understand the emptiness of the object.

Our use of the term *ultimate mind* might suggest that at least *that* mind exists ultimately, but by the same process of seeking it, we will see that this too cannot exist objectively, from its own side, without relying on other factors.

This applies to all phenomena, even emptiness itself. We might possibly conclude that all other phenomena, because they rely on causes and conditions to come into being (or whatever reasoning we use), are empty of intrinsic existence, but then think that surely emptiness, as the final mode of existence, does not rely on other factors, making it the one candidate for ultimate existence.[44] A Madhyamaka philosopher would argue that if emptiness existed ultimately, then when analyzed by an ultimate mind, its intrinsic nature would be found. Yet that is not the case. When an ultimate mind analyzes its final mode of existence, the conclusion is that even emptiness is totally devoid of ultimate existence.

For an object to exist ultimately, according to Madhyamaka scholars, it would also have to exist *without needing to be ascertained by a nondefective awareness*. An ultimately existent object must exist objectively, whether or not a mind apprehends it. The "book-ness" of the book must be an intrinsic part of the book, completely independent of the mind observing it.

This is not so. The book is a collection of parts; its "book-ness" is merely a label that the mind attaches to it. It does not come from the book's side at all. Therefore, for that book to exist as a book depends on mind, and that mind must be a correct mind—a *nondefective aware-ness*. This is to distinguish it from perceptions that are mistaken, such as when we squint and see two moons where there is only one.

## ULTIMATE TRUTH

Ultimate truth is a subject that has occupied the greatest scholars for centuries, because according to Prasangika Madhyamaka, it is the final mode of existence of all phenomena. In *Illumination of the Thought*, Lama Tsongkhapa says:

> A phenomenon found by a valid consciousness perceiving the meaning of reality is an ultimate truth.[45]

Scholars such as Lama Tsongkhapa, his student Khedrup Je, and Changkya Rolpai Dorje (1717–86) have all defined ultimate truth in their own terms, but the core of their definitions is that an ultimate truth is an object found by a valid consciousness that realizes the ultimate.

For Prasangikas, emptiness is called ultimate truth for the following reasons:

+ It is an object because it is findable by a wisdom in meditative equipoise.

+ It is ultimate because it is the object's real mode of existence.

+ It is a truth because there is concordance between its appearance and its mode of existence.

Let's look at the points above in relation to the final mode of existence of the body. Unanalyzed, the body instinctively appears to us as a single causeless entity, whereas when we do analyze it, we see that it is nothing more than a label placed on a collection of constantly changing parts, each a product of causes and conditions, and so it lacks any true, concrete, inherent existence whatsoever.

This ultimate truth is an object (the first point above) because it can be found by an ultimate mind analyzing suchness. This lack of inherent existence is the actual mode of existence of the object, the body (the second point), and the mind that realizes that mode of existence is completely free from any fault regarding the object, so this is its ultimate truth (the third point). It is also a truth because the way it exists and the way it appears to the mind of a superior being—one able to realize emptiness directly—are the same.

Having presented a general overview of the two truths according to the two subschools of the Madhyamaka, I would now like to look in more detail in the next chapter at what the Prasangika scholars say about relationship between the two truths. A deep understanding of both how things appear to us—conventional truth—and how they exist—ultimate truth—is needed to really free us from our most deep-seated problems, and this is what all the preceding chapters have been leading to.

# 7 ILLUSION AND REALITY

## The Relationship Between the Two Truths

IT MIGHT SEEM that relative truth and ultimate truth are two completely unrelated things, but this is not so. This is something that Madhyamaka scholars discuss in depth, as it is regarded as a vital point in understanding the subtle line between illusion and reality.

The three lower schools also discuss the relationship between the two truths, but their assertions fall short of the critical and intimate relationship asserted by the Madhyamikas. For the lower schools, objects exist as real, and upon them is placed one characteristic: selflessness or emptiness.

According to Madhyamaka proponents, the relationship between the two truths could not be closer. For any phenomenon, its relative truth and ultimate truth represent different aspects of that phenomenon. For a book, the object itself is the relative truth and its emptiness is the ultimate truth. It is stated that the two truths are *one entity but different isolates*. We will consider these two terms in the next section.

First, we need to be clear that conventional truth and ultimate truth are *not* the same. They are, in fact, mutually exclusive. My body has these two truths: It *is* a conventional truth, but it *has* an ultimate truth. There is no phenomenon that is both a conventional truth and an ultimate truth. This implies that any phenomenon that exists must be either one or the other. There is nothing that is both, and there is nothing that is neither.

At present we see all things as existing intrinsically; therefore, we cannot see that they are empty of intrinsic or inherent existence. When we have developed sufficiently and can perceive emptiness directly, we will be able to see all things as lacking inherent existence and hence will no longer see things as existing inherently. That is what *mutually exclusive* means in this instance.

By realizing the lack of inherent existence, inherent existence is excluded. Because conventional truth and ultimate truth are mutually exclusive, while our mind is realizing the conventional reality of our sense of "I," at that moment the ultimate reality of our sense of "I" cannot arise, and vice versa. When we reach a stage where we realize the final mode of existence of our "I"—which is its absence of inherent existence, its emptiness or ultimate truth—we cannot simultaneously have a mind that realizes the conventional reality of our "I."

That is the point. Understanding that my body is impermanent will immediately stop my grasping at it as permanent, because these two are mutually exclusive phenomena. If we could actually realize that the body is a product (*product* and *impermanent* are identical in all but terminology) in that it has been produced by causes and conditions, that would go a long way toward eliminating attachment to the body, simply because the two minds cannot exist simultaneously. They are mutually exclusive.

Of course this process of understanding impermanence is not like a light switch, either off or on. It must happen slowly, through effort, with moments of realization becoming gradually more prevalent. Slowly we will come to know the impermanence of our body or our sense of "I," and slowly we will lose our habit of grasping on to its permanence as the opposing habit becomes stronger.

I would like to ask a movie director how he sees his movies. Does he get just as wrapped up in them as does the audience? Does he actually feel that what is happening is real? Or does the process of spending hours and hours just for one short sequence mean that he will always look at what is on the screen and be distant from it? While we are in tears, he will be looking at the way it was lit, whether the camera was in focus, or how well the actors were acting.

The classical example we use in Buddhism is a magician creating his magic, which we have already talked about. The magician knows the tricks he is using, but the audience is fooled into thinking that his illusions are real. Similarly, a buddha sees things quite differently from how we see things. He or she can see that things do not exist in the way they appear. As long as we grasp at an object, its appearance and its real existence will always be discordant with one another, and there will never be any room for them to match up.

Many great masters such as Nagarjuna say that enormous fear arises as our sense of "I" and its real mode of existence become closer. As our meditations take us closer to the way the "I" actually exists, the conventional sense of "I" diminishes. Because these two understandings are mutually exclusive, it is as if the "I" is disappearing, although of course this is not what is really happening. The false grasping at a sense of intrinsic identity creates fear as we feel we are losing our identity and becoming nonexistent. Of course we are terrified.

"We" are not disappearing. We have clung to that false sense of "I" since beginningless time; it is only natural that it is hard to give it up. It feels like we are becoming nothing when all that is happening is that the appearance of the object and its actual mode of existence are becoming closer. This fear is a symptom of the fact that conventional truth and ultimate truth are mutually exclusive.

## ONE ENTITY, DIFFERENT ISOLATES

Relative truth and ultimate truth are one entity, but that does not mean they are the same. As we have just seen, they are mutually exclusive. For any given phenomenon we can examine either of the two natures and arrive at the conclusion that they are both the same entity. My body, for example, exists; therefore, it must be either a conventional truth or an ultimate truth. But my body *has* both natures. I am not saying it *is* both natures. The existence of my body *is* its conventional truth nature, but it *has* another nature as well—that is, its ultimate truth nature.

My body's relative and ultimate truths are one entity in that it is the same object analyzed in different ways. In other words, the basis of analysis is the same—my body—but the mode of analysis is different. My conventional mind apprehends the conventional truth nature of my body, but my ultimate mind apprehends its lack of inherent existence—its ultimate truth nature.

Using the *same base*, the only difference is the conclusion. Without the same base, there is no way to posit either conventional or ultimate truth; without the base there *is* no conventional or ultimate truth. In that way—because different consciousnesses analyze the same object—the two truths are the same entity.

The two truths are also the same entity in that they have the *same duration*. The conventional truth and ultimate truth of a phenomenon arise, abide, and disintegrate at the same time. There is no sequence in which, for example, a conventional truth is generated and then, as a result of that, at a later time, an ultimate truth is generated.

On the other hand, relative truth and ultimate truth are different *isolates* of one entity. The simplest way to explain this is to say that they are different names for the same thing. Because we approach the same object with a different mind, the object appears differently to us.

Maybe you know your doctor quite well. At the clinic, things are a bit formal, so you call her "Doctor," but when you see her anywhere else, you might call her "Claire." Do you see how there is a different flavor to the same object, depending on the name we give it?

All phenomena have these two mutually exclusive aspects, even emptiness itself. Although it may seem strange that emptiness can have a conventional truth nature as well as an ultimate truth nature, it must be understood that emptiness can *have* a conventional truth nature, not that it *is* a conventional truth.

If one definition of conventional truth is "that which appears in a manner discordant with its real existence," how can that apply to emptiness? All phenomena have both truths, which means that for every existent object there is an emptiness and a base to that emptiness included in one entity. The table is the base and the emptiness of the table is its ultimate truth. For emptiness, there is emptiness as a base, but then we must also posit the emptiness of emptiness as its ultimate truth. That emptiness base serves as the conventional truth to the emptiness of emptiness that is the ultimate truth.

We are starting to understand emptiness now, but we are still using our worldly mind. Our knowledge of emptiness is itself a conventional truth. At this stage, even though we can intellectually understand the point, we don't actually "see" emptiness as lacking inherent existence. As a conventional truth it must serve as a base for its own ultimate truth, its emptiness. To a deluded mind, even emptiness itself appears truly existent.

## THE FAULTS IF THE TWO TRUTHS WERE DIFFERENT ENTITIES

In the *Sutra Unraveling the Thought*, the Buddha talks about the faults that would occur if the two truths were either different entities or one isolate. If they were different entities, then, by realizing emptiness:

+ We would still not overcome the conception of true existence.
+ The emptiness of an object would not be the final mode of existence of that object.
+ The emptiness of an object—that which excludes the true existence of that object—would not reach its true nature.
+ Buddhas would see objects as truly existent.

Ultimate truth and conventional truth are differentiated only because of the mind apprehending them. An ultimate mind analyzing emptiness ascertains the object's ultimate truth, whereas a conventional mind apprehends the object's conventional truth. This would not be the case if the two truths were different entities.

Because they are mutually exclusive but one entity, understanding emptiness eliminates the misunderstanding that it inherently exists. If the two were different entities, like teapot and cup, this whole argument would fall apart. Realizing the emptiness of the teapot would not eliminate the misunderstanding about the cup.

Lama Tsongkhapa has an expression: Your target is in the east but you are aiming at the west. We want to find the true mode of existence of an object that is in the east, yet we are looking for it in the west.

Similarly, if conventional and ultimate truth were different entities, then the object (one entity) and its absence of inherent existence (the other entity) would be two totally different things. This would mean that the emptiness of true existence of the object would not be its final mode of abiding. So it would follow that we could not use a mind of ultimate analysis to analyze the ultimate nature of an object because the base under analysis would be completely different. It would be like trying to get at the nature of water by analyzing a lump of wood.

If conventional truth and ultimate truth were different entities, then the third fault would be that our realization analyzing the final nature of things and events would not reach the final realization, the realization of emptiness. Emptiness is a nonaffirming negation; it negates true existence without presuming something else positive in its place. This is different from an affirming negation, such as the statement "My friend is not a man," which assumes that she is a woman. If the two truths were different entities, then realizing the lack of inherent existence of an object would not be able to counteract the mind's intuitive belief in that object's inherent existence. This would mean, for example, that when meditators meditate on the final mode of existence of an object, they would not reach an understanding of the emptiness of true existence, because there would be no connection between the object and its final mode of existence.

Finally, there is a fault in seeing the two truths as different entities because then the buddhas would not be able to directly realize the two truths simultaneously and would consequently see objects as truly existent. The buddhas would not simultaneously and directly perceive an object and that object's emptiness of true existence. But this is not the case. One of the consequences of an object's conventional side and ultimate side being the same entity is that the buddhas do indeed perceive these two natures simultaneously in one object.

Conversely, if the two truths were one isolate, common beings like us would directly realize the true mode of existence, and yet we would still be unable to overcome afflictions even as we are directly perceiving reality.

## How Things Exist

### THE TRUTH THAT CONCEALS

A conventional or concealer truth—this "truth that conceals"—creates a fictitious world that works for us on a certain level. We catch trains that are very real to us; we eat food that is very real to us. We have a strong sense of what's real and what's not. The television news is real, but Batman is not. Apart from some blurred edges where we are not sure about the reality of things, generally we feel we can easily distinguish between reality and fiction.

Nevertheless, at one level it is all fiction. Our "real" world might cause us pleasure or tears that somehow seem on a different level from the pleasure or tears that a soap opera on television causes us, but at another level they are both fiction. In spite of this, in the relative world of conventionalities, all things and events, including our own sense of self, appear very independent or solid. According to the Madhyamaka school, all sentient beings possess this ignorance equally.

Because of this ignorance I can see, feel, and function. I can do things, I can communicate, I can conceptualize. This conceptual mind is not necessarily a negative mind. We need concepts to understand reality. We are using concepts now. They can help us reduce our ignorance, but they are not the final solution. The real solution will come from direct perception, not from our conceptual mind. We are, however, a long way from having yogic direct perceptions of the world, and to us, at this moment, the conventional world is all there is.

We currently live in a familiar world entirely imbued with our ignorant view. If we get rid of our ignorance, then what sort of world are we going to have? Will we become robots? This is a challenging question. Life, feeling, and communication only seem to happen within the sphere of relative truth, so does that mean that ultimate reality is nothingness?

It is said that the Madhyamaka school's philosophical view is right on the brink of nihilism. Tibetan masters often use the term "standing on the edge of a sword." The masters tell us that realizing ultimate truth is not like having been in a dark room that immediately becomes bright when we switch on the light. The ignorance I possess within me won't disappear instantly, in just a moment. This ignorance will be removed through the process of gradually substituting other non-ignorant minds. We slowly eliminate our delusions until we reach the state of cessation, which is liberation or enlightenment. And an enlightened being is definitely not like a stone.

## How Things Exist Conventionally

The Prasangikas' key assertion that all things and events lack any intrinsic or inherent nature is such a subtle one that confusion can easily arise regarding the difference between inherent existence and existence itself. While agreeing that things lack true existence, Svatantrika masters like Bhavavevika insist that there must be some essential nature and that to assert the lack of inherent existence is to assert non-existence. Because of that Lama Tsongkhapa says in the *Great Treatise on the Stages of the Path*:

> As this [refuting conventional existence as posited by lower schools] is extremely difficult, accurate understanding of the presentation of the two truths hardly exists.[46]

To begin to understand how the Prasangikas assert that things and events exist, it is necessary to differentiate between conventional *truth* and *conventional* existence. As I have said, to exist *ultimately* is to exist independently, truly, so nothing exists in that way. But to exist *conventionally* is to exist dependent on causes and conditions. That empty interdependence is the mode of existence of all things, including all conventional truths and ultimate truths.

As we saw in the previous chapter, the division between the subschools comes with the most subtle view of existence, that of inherent existence. While both agree on the above with regard to conventional existence, the Prasangikas assert further that ultimate existence and inherent existence are synonyms.[47] Since this distinction is such a fine one, and since the other schools see *lack of inherent existence* as *nonexistence* it is incumbent on the Prasangikas to explain exactly how things *do* exist conventionally. This is clearly explained by Lama Tsongkhapa in the *Great Treatise on the Stages of the Path*:

> How does one determine whether something exists conventionally? We assert that something exists conventionally if:
> 1. It is known to a conventional consciousness.
> 2. No other conventional valid cognition contradicts it being so known.
> 3. Reason that accurately analyzes the reality of whether something inherently exists does not contradict it.
>
> We hold anything that fails to meet these criteria as nonexistent.[48]

According to the Prasangika Madhyamaka, says Lama Tsongkhapa, phenomena must possess these three criteria to exist conventionally. Not only must something be an object of a conventional consciousness, that consciousness must not be invalidated by another conventional valid cognition, nor by a mind analyzing its final mode of existence, its emptiness. Without these three criteria, a phenomenon cannot be said to conventionally exist.

The conventional consciousness of the first criterion is also called *mundane knowledge*, in the sense that it is the knowledge or consciousness that occurs in all people. It is a "nonanalytical" consciousness. This does not mean that such a consciousness never analyzes anything but that the consciousness does not analyze the final mode of existence of things and events. To be "known to a conventional consciousness" means a nonanalytical consciousness posits the existence of a thing through perception and language. Quite simply, we know an object through our senses, and that is about as far as it goes. Not all objects of conventional consciousnesses exist, however, so this criterion is not sufficient to determine the existence of an object.

The second criterion is that the first cognition is not contradicted by any other conventional valid cognition. It is perfectly possible for something to be known to a conventional mundane consciousness but not actually exist. There are many cultural things, good or bad, right or wrong, philosophical or religious, that are based on the construction of conventional language and that are believed to exist but in reality do not. Many of us, for example, have a strong unconscious belief that death will not come for at least a few years or a few decades. That nonanalytical consciousness is contradicted by another valid cognition. Through analysis we can ascertain the fact that the time of our death is utterly uncertain and that we might actually die at any moment. The belief that we will not is erroneous and can be contradicted by valid reasoning.

Many tourists to London go to Baker Street looking for Sherlock Holmes' house. Although these people actually believe there was a Sherlock Holmes, and he is a very well-known "object of cognition," their belief is not valid. Although Sherlock Holmes is well known to the worldly mind, he does not exist. A valid consciousness is needed to actually see this crucial difference between what does and what does not exist. Sherlock Holmes's existence can be disputed by a valid consciousness.

The third criterion matches the conventional consciousness with another consciousness that analyzes whether the object inherently exists. This first consciousness must not be contradicted by the second. The most obvious object that is thus contradicted is the belief in inherent existence itself. In another example, Lama Tsongkhapa explains that an ultimate mind will not contradict the conventional assertion that pleasure and pain arise conventionally from positive and negative actions, whereas it will contradict the conventional assertion that pleasure and pain arise from a creator god or a primal essence.

Apart from someone who has realized emptiness directly and who is trained in the philosophical tenets, everyone lives with the sense that things have an inherent nature. Therefore, only this third criterion will cover all possibilities, and unless an object fulfills all three criteria, then it cannot be said to exist conventionally.

## The Sequence of Realizing the Two Truths

In chapter 6 of his *Supplement to the Middle Way*, Chandrakirti says:

> Except for the path explained by the great master Nagarjuna,
> There is no [other] way to reach transcendent peace.
> All others fail to grasp the truths of the ultimate and of the
>    conventional,
> And therefore liberation lies beyond their reach.
>
> Conventional truths are the methods,
> And ultimate truths arise from that method.
> Those who fail to see how these two differ
> Are mistaken in thought and therefore take mistaken paths.[49]

As we have seen, Chandrakirti wrote his *Supplement* as a commentary on Nagarjuna's *Fundamental Treatise on the Middle Way*. These two verses clearly show that for people who do not understand Nagarjuna's view it is extremely difficult to experience peace. Here peace can be seen on two levels. First, it is the complete cessation of suffering, which from the two lower schools' perspective refers to those who achieve arhatship, or freedom from samsara, and from the Mahayana perspective refers to those followers of the bodhisattva path who have achieved the eighth *bhumi*[50] and beyond.

The second verse shows that there is some kind of sequence. The realization or understanding of conventional truth is the method to understand and cultivate ultimate truth. Unless we know this fully and completely, we will experience difficulties on the spiritual path.

Therefore, it is extremely important to know the two truths fully, but particularly the two truths as explained by Nagarjuna, because, as I hope has been made clear by now, the various Buddhist (and many non-Buddhist) philosophical schools all have explanations of the two truths. To experience the peace of liberation takes great subtlety of understanding, and that, says Chandrakirti, requires a thorough understanding of Nagarjuna's profound exposition.

Which realization will come first, conventional truth or ultimate truth? The second verse states very clearly that conventional truths are the method and ultimate truths arise from that method. Here, it is important to know that it is *not* saying that emptiness arises from conventional truth, but that an understanding of conventional truth will help in developing an understanding of ultimate truth. Thus, the former is the method to achieve the latter. On an objective level, conventional truth is the base and ultimate truth is a feature of that base. The main focus here, however, is not the objective aspect but the subjective. Understanding conventional truth will help us achieve the understanding of ultimate truth.

Here, we need some clarification. It is correct, and we can certainly assert, that understanding ultimate truth arises from understanding conventional truth. There are, however, different levels of understanding of conventional truth. Knowing an object is different from knowing the conventional truth of that object. Take my mala rosary as an example. It is a conventional truth because there is a disparity between its appearance and its real existence. I have had it for many years and I know it intimately; it has 108 beads, it has this particular color, there are four beads that are slightly chipped. There is a very valid understanding in my head that this is *my* mala, and nobody can prove otherwise. But is knowing an object this thoroughly sufficient to have an understanding of the object's conventional truth? Or do we need something more?

The conventional truth of the mala is not the collection of facts above. It is that the mala appears to my consciousness as having inherent existence and that this is how my consciousness apprehends it. For this reason, in order to understand a conventional truth, we first need to understand an object's ultimate truth, that is, we need first to determine its lack of inherent existence.

This may sound contradictory, but we are not dealing here with conventional *knowledge* of a conventional object, but an understanding of the conventional *truth* of that object. That is the difference. Lama Tsongkhapa, in *Illumination of the Thought*, says that finding concealer truths will not happen until we have found the middle way—that is, emptiness—because to establish something as a concealer truth we are actually establishing its false nature, the sense that it is inherently existent. This can only be done through refutation when we have found its true mode of existence, its lack of inherent existence. To say that an object exists inherently only according to ignorance implies that the object does not exist inherently in actuality.

We now have to reconcile two statements that appear to be contradictory: first, that we need to understand ultimate truths before conventional truths, and second, that conventional truths are methods to help us realize ultimate truths. The crucial word here is "realize." It is very true that we can't understand the conventional nature of an object—that it appears to exist inherently when it does not—before we have an understanding of its lack of inherent nature, but that does not mean we must first directly realize emptiness. The two truths, in fact, help each other. When we walk we use both legs, first one and then the other. In the same way, a fairly gross understanding of ultimate truth takes our understanding of conventional truth to a deeper level, then that level of understanding of conventional truth takes our understanding of ultimate truth to a deeper level, and so on.

In this way, our understanding of conventional truths will lead us finally to a deep direct realization of the ultimate truth of emptiness. Before that, however, we must use our conceptual, logical understanding of emptiness to realize that the object we are exploring is a conventional truth because it appears to have inherent existence whereas it does not.

This subtle level of conventional truth, wherein the object appears to have an inherent existence that it in fact does not have, will only be realized *after* we have a fairly good understanding of ultimate truth. So, even though Chandrakirti is quite correct in asserting that conventional truths are the method and ultimate truths arise from that method, in the actual mechanics of realizing both conventional and ultimate truth, the order is reversed.

## How Realized Beings Perceive Relative Truths

Do all conventional truths—the things and events that make up our universe—appear to every living being's mind as having true nature? It is said in the texts that while this is certainly so for ordinary beings, it is not the case for the two kinds of arhats—hearers (*shravakas*) and solitary realizers (*pratyekabuddhas*)—and for bodhisattvas above the eighth bhumi. When those highly realized beings perceive conventional truths, they do not perceive them as having a truly existent nature because they have already abandoned the ignorant mind that conceals the ultimate truth of those conventional truths. For all others below the eighth bhumi of the bodhisattva's path, they subjectively perceive things and events as having true nature, and the objects themselves objectively appear to them as having true nature. Therefore, to those beings these objects are conventional truths.

When highly realized (but still unenlightened) beings are analyzing the ultimate nature of reality, they do not perceive conventional truths at all, because ultimate truths and conventional truths are mutually exclusive. A practitioner meditating on emptiness will perceive only emptiness; the conventional world will cease during the meditation. The two minds cannot come together in one moment of time. Outside of meditation, when a bodhisattva sees an object, there is still a mistaken consciousness, although the bodhisattva is not fooled by the mistake as we are.

A buddha is a perfected being, utterly without mistaken consciousnesses, and from the moment of his or her enlightenment, there is no time when a buddha does not recognize emptiness directly. As this excludes conventional truths, it raises the quandary that buddhas must, therefore, be unable to see our world and our suffering.

Lama Tsongkhapa explains this seeming contradiction by asserting that buddhas can see conventional truths but *only* from the viewpoint of unenlightened beings, in the same way as a psychiatrist hears a story told by a schizophrenic and yet still does not believe it. Of course, Lama Tsongkhapa does not use the example of the psychiatrist—they are a Western invention—but he talks of how in order to cure an illness, a doctor must know the illness without actually having it.

Omniscience means knowing everything, both the correct and incorrect ways in which things are perceived. A buddha can see the emptiness of a cup and, at the same time, see the way that the cup appears as inherently existing to sentient beings.

## Illusion and Reality

Although due to singing, playing music, and crying
Sounds of echoes arise,
The echo does not reside in the sounds.
Just so you must comprehend all phenomena.

When a man who makes love in a dream
Awakens, he does not see his lover.
Childishly, the lustful still clings to her.
Just so you must comprehend all phenomena.

The magician conjures images
Of horses, elephants, chariots, and so on,
Yet none are as real as they appear to you.
Just so you must comprehend all phenomena.

The eager woman who experiences a dream
Of both the birth and death of a son
Is joyful at the birth and saddened by the death.
Just so you must comprehend all phenomena.[51]

These beautiful verses from the *King of Concentration Sutra*
(*Samadhiraja Sutra*) draw our attention to the fundamental fact of
phenomenal existence, how our confused mind grasps at a substantial reality of things although in actual fact things are empty of inherent being.

There is a discernible degree of fictionalizing in our everyday reality. The object is *there*, and our understanding of the object is *here*, and whether we get close to the truth or are a million miles from it, still we never quite see things as they actually are. The Tibetan masters urge us to see all things as *illusion-like*. Note that they do *not* suggest we see life as an illusion. Life is not a dream with no reality at all, but rather it is *like* a dream, in that, based on the fact, we create the fiction. Of course, many things in our lives we know to be illusions, but they seem quite distinct from the hard reality we live with, as different as a fairytale from a news item.

The *King of Concentration Sutra* takes an echo, a dream, and a magician's illusion as examples of the confusion between appearance and reality. All of these exist conventionally, but what is their status? When we shout in a cave, there is an echo, and we can't dispute its existence. A dream is a process of the mind, so that too exists conventionally.

A magician can make us see an object as something else entirely, in the same way that conditions alter our perception. Taking a rock, the magician casts a spell, and we see a real horse in front of us. If the magician is proficient enough, we will actually believe it. Similarly, everyday objects deceive us because the conditions are there for things to appear to have an intrinsic nature they don't actually have. A book appears as a book to our mind when somebody has bound the pages together and we conventionally agree that this is a book, nothing more. There is nothing from the book's side that defines it as a book.

That things appear in a certain way because of karmic imprints is illustrated by the example of a dream. Dreams are not real, of course, but still, most of the time, they have a very strong connection with our life. Past events, future plans, and fears appear to us in dreams all jumbled up, seemingly without relevance or order, but they are all triggered by the preoccupations and psychological tendencies of our mind. In the same way, we misconceive reality because we have had these karmic seeds from many lifetimes. We are so familiar with seeing everything as inherently existent that we keep seeing things in the same way; it is our deepest habit.

The example of the man desiring his dream-lover illustrates that we are deceived by our emotions. Although lacking any real existence, the dream-woman takes on significance only because of his desire. Perhaps we can't say that we *desire* to see everything intrinsically, but this fundamental need to reify the "I" causes us to see everything as inherently existent.

For a woman to dream of having a child and then develop attachment for that dream-child is absurd. For her to then grieve the death of that dream-child is even more absurd. And yet we develop attachment, aversion, hatred, grief, and so on all the time, based on the sense of permanence that is as divorced from reality as that dream-child.

The echo symbolizes our own habitual tendency to see things as existing independently. The dream-lover takes it that one step further, illustrating how our desire for permanence strengthens this misapprehension: We want things to be permanent, so we see them that way. The magician symbolizes the external conditions that make us misapprehend reality, and the joy and grief that the woman feels for her dream-son shows us the insubstantiality of the objects of our attachment, aversion, and ignorance.

Our reflection in the mirror isn't our real face; the echo isn't our real voice, the person we make love to in a dream isn't our real lover. To us they seem illusions. On the other hand, the world we live in— our body, our possessions, the buildings and streets of our town—seem to be very real. It is difficult for us to understand that they do not exist as they appear to us. Water appears to us as water and we believe it really is water; but when we see our face in a mirror, we understand it is not really our face, just a reflection. For the "unreal" objects we can differentiate quite easily between appearance and reality, but in the case of "real" objects it is much more difficult.

As we have seen, however, according to the Prasangika school there is no difference between these two groups of objects. There is no difference between the reflection of our face and our real face, between what from our worldly perspective we would call "illusion" and "reality." Perhaps a small child might be confused, thinking that the mirror holds her real face, but that is something she will quickly grow out of. From the ultimate perspective, both are equally conventionally existent—one as a reflection, one as a face. There is no difference between them in terms of the way they exist.

The Prasangika scholars are cautioning us that life is not as black and white as it appears. Reality is not as real as it seems, nor is illusion quite as unreal. We need to let go of that sense of concrete reality and see all things as illusion-like. To understand this discordance between appearance and reality on the level we are talking about here requires an understanding of emptiness. Only with such an understanding will we be able to see that appearance is the sense of intrinsic existence whereas reality is the lack of intrinsic existence.

There are different levels of understanding we must all pass through to get to a deeper understanding of emptiness. In a sense, this is what our examination of the four schools within the study of the two truths is all about. By bringing the mind to a more and more subtle level of understanding, we can finally understand its final mode of existence.

This final mode of existence of an object is the lack of inherent existence from its own side. Perhaps this is an idea that sits easily with you, and you can logically accept it, but I am certain that this truth has yet to penetrate to a deeper level. Check for yourself. Do you live your life as if everything in your world lacks intrinsic existence? Are you totally free from clinging to things and events? Would there be not even the slightest ripple in your calm if you lost all your possessions and all your friends turned against you? If the answer is no, then, like all of us, you have a way to go.

By misapprehending the base of designation, we suffer. Take the very traditional example of the coiled rope and the snake. You are walking along a road where there are rumored to be many poisonous snakes. You see a rope in the dark, coiled in exactly the same way a snake might be. Instantly, you experience great fear. Your life is in danger! That fear is real, isn't it? It might only last a few moments until you realize it is just a rope, but until something happens to clear up the situation, your fear is there. The basis of designation is the coiled rope, but we label it *snake*, and fear arises because of that. Attachment, aversion, and ignorance all stem from this same kind of misunderstanding.

Knowing how people, actions, and events exist conventionally makes it possible to understand the four noble truths on a very profound level, and this understanding helps us to generate compassion and so on. We all share this illness of fictionalizing the world we live in. All suffering arises from this misapprehension, and if we can see this, we will stop ascribing good and bad, and meting out our compassion only to those we feel deserve it.

Clearly, differentiating between the fiction our conceptual mind creates and the reality of our life will help us understand the processes of all things and events, how they go together, how they work together.

## Wisdom or Dogma?

All four Buddhist philosophical schools explore the nature of reality. In fact, most philosophies and most religions address this most important question. When you first came across Buddhism and the terms *emptiness* or *shunyata* popped up in your reading, it all probably seemed very esoteric and intellectual. Now that you have had a taste of what each school thinks of as real and fiction, I strongly advise you to reexamine each and see how relevant each one is to your life.

We can approach any philosophy for many reasons. We can study for *religious* reasons, in order to progress spiritually in some way. Or it can be for *epistemological* reasons, in order to understand how the mind operates. On the other hand, there could be an *ontological* bias to our investigations, exploring the nature of reality for its own sake. It might also be because we are suffering in some way and want to explore the mind to find a way out of our suffering, so the study of the mind could be for *therapeutic* reasons.

I suspect, if you are like most people, it will be a mixture of these reasons. That's not a bad thing, but as I said at the very beginning, study for the sake of knowledge alone is relatively meaningless. Knowledge *per se* is just facts accumulated in the way that we accumulate money or CDs. It's what we do with that knowledge that is the important thing. Furthermore, knowledge without either a spiritual or a therapeutic motivation can so easily lead to ego enhancement. There are wonderful, knowledgeable people in the world, but there are also many puffed-up ego-driven "experts," who tend to dictate and advise without a shred of compassion.

You are probably neither Tibetan nor Indian, and this is not simply a question of religious dogma for you. Quite often I wish I were a Westerner, not because I want the trappings of a Westerner, but to have an opportunity to study these things with a mind that is really open and untainted, that has not been flavored by a native bias toward Tibetan Buddhism. I have been trained from childhood in the viewpoint of the Prasangika school, and it is like breathing to me, so much so that I find it impossible to take on any other perspective without the Prasangika angle coloring whatever I am thinking about. Philosophically speaking, you are still relatively unformed, and so you have choices that I don't. Maybe you are a natural Chittamatrin! These topics, in my opinion, are essential to our very well-being and the well-being of the planet; they need serious consideration. For that reason, a new, clear mind is a wonderful asset.

This philosophy can seem quite bewildering, not just because of the mind-bending complexity of the philosophical arguments, but because the final answer seems to be an absence. We look and look and we find a hole! Why is the only true mind one that recognizes the *absence* of independent existence of the object? Because that mind is the only one that is *free from fault*. That is why we use the word *emptiness*. The final wisdom realizes the lack of intrinsic existence of whatever object it is meditating on—the body, the "I," an external object, even emptiness itself. There is no fault at all in that wisdom.

This is what you need to investigate deeply; you need to ascertain in your own mind whether this is a real truth or some kind of religious dogma. Buddhism is millennia old, and what I am giving you is a (hopefully) comprehensible distillation of texts that in direct translation would be very dense and possibly even indecipherable. These texts, steeped in religion, have the flavor of the monastic system they were designed for, so it is easy to see this as wondrously complex, even fascinating, but still just dogma for the indoctrinated. You might even conclude that this is religion whereas Jung or Marx is truth. Please investigate this very seriously. The deeper you understand and sympathize with the philosophies of the various schools, the stronger your motivation will be to truly use this wisdom to turn your life around.

# Glossary

ABHIDHARMA (Skt.): the collected teachings on metaphysics and wisdom among the three "baskets" of teachings of the Buddha.

AGGREGATES, THE FIVE: the traditional Buddhist division of body and mind. The five are form, feeling, discrimination, compositional factors, and consciousness.

ANATMAN (Skt.): *no-self*; the Buddha's explanation on selflessness, as opposed to the prevailing non-Buddhist doctrine of *atman* (*self*).

ARHAT (Skt.): a practitioner who has achieved the state of no more learning in the individual liberation vehicle.

ARYA (Skt.): a superior being, one who has gained a direct realization of emptiness.

ATMAN (Skt.): *self*. See anatman

BHUMI (Skt.): *level*, one of ten levels of realization that a bodhisattva passes through to reach enlightenment.

BODHICHITTA (Skt.): the mind that spontaneously wishes to attain enlightenment in order to benefit others; the fully open and dedicated heart.

BODHISATTVA (Skt.): someone whose spiritual practice is directed toward the achievement of enlightenment for the welfare of all beings; one who possesses the compassionate motivation of bodhichitta.

BÖN (Tib.): the religion prevalent in Tibet before Buddhism; many aspects of it were assimilated into Tibetan Buddhism.

BUDDHA, A (Skt.): a fully enlightened being; one who has removed all obscurations veiling the mind and developed all good qualities to perfection; the first of the Three Jewels of refuge.

BUDDHA, THE (Skt.): the historical buddha, Shakyamuni.

BUDDHADHARMA (Skt.): the Buddha's teachings.

CHITTAMATRA (Skt.): the Mind-Only school; the third of the four Buddhist philosophical schools studied in Tibetan Buddhism.

CONCEALER TRUTH: a synonym for conventional or relative truth, indicating that although something is relatively true, it conceals the deeper truth that all things are empty of inherent existence.

DEPENDENT ARISING: origination in dependence on causes and conditions.

DESIRE REALM: Buddhist cosmology posits three realms within samsara, the desire, form, and formless realms. The first includes all the six realms of hell beings, hungry ghosts, animals, humans, demigods, and gods. The other two, the form and formless realms, are entered by yogis who have developed deep states of meditative concentration in their previous lives.

DHARMA (Skt.): literally "that which holds (one back from suffering)"; often refers to the Buddha's teachings, but more generally to anything that helps the practitioner attain liberation; the second of the Three Jewels of refuge.

DHARMAKAYA (Skt.): *See* truth body

EMPTINESS (Skt. *shunyata*): the ultimate nature of all phenomena, which is their lack of any inherent or independent existence.

EPISTEMOLOGY: the study of how the mind acquires and validates knowledge; specifically in Buddhism, the study of the nature of the mind.

ETERNALISM: believing things and events to exist independently, from their own side.

FORM BODY (Skt. *rupakaya*): one of the two buddha bodies achieved when one attains enlightenment; the result of the method side of practice. This can further be divided into the enjoyment body (Skt. *sambhogakaya*) and the emanation body (Skt. *nirmanakaya*).

FORM REALM. *See* desire realm

FOUR NOBLE TRUTHS, THE: the subject of the first discourse of the Buddha; the four noble truths are: the truth of suffering, the truth of the origin of suffering, the truth of the cessation of suffering, and the truth of the path leading to the cessation of suffering.

GELUG (Tib.): founded by Lama Tsongkhapa, this is one of the four schools of Tibetan Buddhism; the others are Sakya, Nyingma, and Kagyu.

GESHE (Tib.): the title of a teacher in the Gelug sect who has completed the most extensive monastic and philosophical training.

HEARER (Skt. *shravaka*): a practitioner without a bodhichitta motivation who has eliminated his or her suffering through the direct perception of emptiness after listening to the teachings from a qualified master. Hearers are contrasted to solitary realizers, who develop realization and liberation on their own.

INHERENT EXISTENCE: existing from its own side, on a mind labeling it.

KADAM (Tib.): this tradition of Buddhism in Tibet was founded by Atisha around the eleventh century; it was eventually integrated into all four existing traditions within Tibetan Buddhism.

KANGYUR (Tib.): the Tibetan canon of scriptures directly attributed to the Buddha.

KARMA (Skt.): literally, "action"; the natural law of cause and effect whereby positive actions produce happiness and negative actions produce suffering.

KARMIC IMPRINT (Tib. *pakchak*): the energy or propensity left by a mental act on the mindstream that will remain until it either ripens into a result or is purified.

LAMA TSONGKHAPA (1357–1419): a preeminent Tibetan scholar and tantric master and founder of the Gelug tradition.

LAMRIM (Tib.): the graduated path to enlightenment; the progressive presentation of the Buddha's teachings primarily propounded by the Gelug school of Tibetan Buddhism.

MAHAYANA (Skt.): literally, the Great Vehicle; one of the two main divisions of Buddhism. Practiced primarily in Tibet, Mongolia, China, Vietnam, Korea, and Japan, Mahayana Buddhism emphasizes bodhichitta, the wisdom of emptiness (rather than selflessness), and full enlightenment (rather than liberation for oneself alone).

MALA (Tib.): rosary, or prayer beads, used to count recitations of mantras.

NIHILISM: the belief that things have no degree of existence at all.

NIRVANA (Skt.): liberation; a state of freedom from all delusions and karma, and therefore from cyclic existence (*samsara*).

NOBLE EIGHTFOLD PATH, THE: the Buddha's discourse wherein he explains the various attributes we need to develop to attain freedom from suffering; they are right speech, right action, right livelihood, right effort, right mindfulness, right concentration, right view, and right thought.

ONTOLOGY: the study of how things exist.

PALI: the ancient Indian language used in the earliest known Buddhist canonical texts.

PARINIRVANA (Skt.): the state the Buddha achieved at his death.

PERFECTIONS: (Skt. *paramita*); practices "gone beyond" to be perfected by bodhisattvas; they are most commonly enumerated as six: generosity, ethics, patience, joyous effort, concentration, and wisdom.

PITAKA (Skt.): one of three "baskets" of the Buddha's teachings that comprise the Buddhist canon.

PRAJÑAPARAMITA (Skt.): the perfection (*paramita*) of wisdom (*prajña*); the collection of Mahayana sutras explicitly teaching emptiness while implicitly teaching the paths of the bodhisattva. The *Heart Sutra* is an example.

PRAMANA (Skt.): valid cognition; the study of how the mind can know objects incontrovertibly.

PRASANGIKA MADHYAMAKA (Skt.): the Middle Way Consequence school; the higher of the two subschools of the Madhyamaka.

REALIST SCHOOL: refers to the two lower philosophical schools of Buddhism, Vaibhashika and Sautrantika, which see objects as existing from their own side and hence as "real."

SAMADHI (Skt.): the state of meditative equipoise.

SAMKHYA (Skt.): another philosophical system prevalent in India during Buddhism's development there. Like the followers of Brahmanism, the Samkhyas believed in the existence of the atman, or self.

SAMSARA (Skt.): cyclic existence, the state of being repeatedly reborn due to delusions and karma.

SANSKRIT: the ancient Indian language in which most Mahayana texts were composed.

SAUTRANTIKA (Skt.): the Sutra school, the second of the four Buddhist philosophical schools; one of the two realist schools.

SEALS, THE FOUR: the basic Buddhist tenets, also called the *four views* or *four axioms*. They are (1) all compositional phenomena are impermanent, (2) all contaminated things are suffering, (3) all phenomena are empty and selfless, and (4) nirvana is true peace.

SHASTRA (Skt.): a classical Indian treatise on the teachings of the Buddha.

SHUNYATA (Skt.): literally, emptiness.

SOLITARY REALIZER (Skt. *pratyekabuddha*): one who achieves liberation from suffering through practicing in solitude, without following a master. *See also* hearer

SUTRA (Skt.): a discourse of the Buddha.

SUTRAYANA (Skt.): the vehicle of the Mahayana that takes the Buddhist sutras as its main textual source.

SVATANTRIKA MADHYAMAKA (Skt.): the Middle Way Autonomy school, the first subschool of the Madhyamaka.

TANTRA (Skt.): literally, "thread" or "continuity"; a text of esoteric Buddhist teachings; often refers to the practices associated with those texts.

TATHAGATA (Skt.): epithet for the Buddha, meaning "one thus gone."

TENET: a belief or premise of a religion or philosophy.

TENGYUR (Tib.): the Tibetan canon of classical Indian treatises on the Buddha's teachings.

TRUTH BODY (Skt. *dharmakaya*): one of the two buddha bodies achieved when one attains enlightenment; the result of the wisdom side of practice. This can be further divided into the wisdom truth body (Skt. *jñanakaya*) and the natural truth body (Skt. *svabhavikakaya*).

VAJRAYANA (Skt.): literally, "adamantine vehicle"; the vehicle of tantra, also called Mantrayana or Tantrayana.

VAIBHASHIKA (Skt.): the Great Exposition school; the first of the four Buddhist philosophical schools studied in Tibetan Buddhism; one of the two realist schools.

VALID COGNIZER: a mind that apprehends its object correctly and accurately.

VINAYA PITAKA (Skt.): one of the three "baskets" (*pitakas*) of the Buddha's canonical teachings, relating to ethical behavior, such as monastic and lay vows or the administration of monasteries.

# BIBLIOGRAPHY

## Sutras

*Meeting of the Father and Son Sutra* (*Pitaputrasamagama Sutra*). Derge Kangyur, Sutrapitaka, vol. *nga*.

*Descent into Lanka Sutra* (*Lankavatara Sutra*). Derge Kangyur, Sutrapitaka, vol. *ca*.x

## Other Texts

Asanga. *Compendium of Ascertainments* (*Vinishchayasamgrahani*). Derge Tengyur, Chittamatra, vol. *zi*.

Chandrakirti. *Clear Words* (*Prasannapada*). Derge Tengyur, Madhyamaka, vol. *a*.

———. *Supplement to the Middle Way* (*Madhyamakavatara*). Derge Tengyur, Madhyamaka, vol. *a*.

Dharmakirti. *Commentary on [Dignaga's "Compendium on] Valid Cognition"* (*Pramanavarttika*).

Dreyfus, Georges. *Recognizing Reality: Dharmakirti's Philosophy and Its Tibetan Interpretations.* Albany, N.Y.: State University of New York Press, 1997.

Gyatso, Tenzin, the Fourteenth Dalai Lama. *Practicing Wisdom: The Perfection of Shantideva's Bodhisattva Way.* Trans. Geshe Thupten Jinpa. Boston: Wisdom Publications, 2005.

———. *Stages of Meditation.* Ithaca, N.Y.: Snow Lion Publications, 2001.

———. *The World of Tibetan Buddhism.* Trans. Geshe Thupten Jinpa. Boston: Wisdom Publications, 1994.

Jinpa, Thupten. *Self, Reality and Reason in Tibetan Philosophy.* Oxford: RoutledgeCurzon, 2002.

Nagarjuna. *Fundamental Treatise on the Middle Way (Mulamadhya-makakarika).* Derge Tengyur, Madhyamaka, vol. *tsa.*

Newland, Guy. *Appearance and Reality: The Two Truths in the Four Buddhist Tenet Systems.* Ithaca, N.Y.: Snow Lion Publications, 1999.

———. *The Two Truths.* Ithaca, N.Y.: Snow Lion Publications, 1992.

Pabongka Rinpoche. *Liberation in the Palm of Your Hand.* Boston: Wisdom Publications, 1991 (revised edition, 2006).

Purnavardhana. *Lakshanusarini* (a commentary on Vasubandhu's *Treasury of Abhidharma*). Derge Tengyur, Abhidharma, vol. *zhu.*

Shantideva. *A Guide to the Bodhisattva's Way of Life (Bodhicharya-vatara).* Trans. Stephen Batchelor. Dharamsala, India: Library of Tibetan Works and Archives, 1981.

Tagore, Rabindranath. *An Anthology.* London: Picador, 1997.

Tsering, Geshe Tashi. *Buddhist Psychology.* Boston: Wisdom Publications, 2006.

———. *The Four Noble Truths.* Boston: Wisdom Publications, 2005.

Tsongkhapa. *Great Treatise on the Stages of the Path to Enlightenment (Byang chub lam rim che ba).* Zi-ling: Tso Ngon People's Press, 1985. Translated into English in three volumes by the Lamrim Chenmo Translation Committee as Tsong-kha-pa. *The Great Treatise on the Stages of the Path to Enlightenment: The Lamrim Chenmo.* Ithaca, N.Y.: Snow Lion Publications, 2000–2004.

————. *Illumination of the Thought: An Extensive Explanation of Chandrakirti's "Supplement to the Middle Way"* (*Dgongs pa rab gsal*). Sarnath, India: The Pleasure of Elegant Sayings Press, 1973.

————(rJe Tsong khapa). *Ocean of Reasoning: A Great Commentary on Nagarjuna's Mulamadhyamakakarika.* Trans. Geshe Ngawang Samten and Jay L. Garfield. Oxford: Oxford University Press, 2006. Tibetan text: Sarnath, India: The Pleasure of Elegant Sayings Press, 1992.

————. *Ocean of Eloquence: Tsong kha pa's Commentary on the Yogacara Doctrine of Mind.* Trans. Gareth Sparham. Albany, N.Y.: State University of New York Press, 1993.

Vasubandhu. *Treasury of Valid Knowledge* (*Abhidharmakosha*). Sarnath, India: the Pleasure of Elegant Sayings Press, 1973.

————. *Autocommentary on the Treasury of Higher Knowledge* (*Abhidharmakoshabhashyam*). Derge Tengyur, Abhidharma, vol. *chu*.

Vasumitra. *Commentary on the "Treasure of Abhidharma"* (*Abhidharmakoshatika*). Derge Tengyur, Abhidharma, vol. *chu*.

# NOTES

SOME QUOTATIONS in the text are translations by Geshe Tashi Tsering of the edition of the Kangyur (the Tibetan canon of the scriptures attributed to the Buddha) and Tengyur (the Tibetan canon of the classical treatises primarily by Indian masters) published at Derge. These references cite the thematic section of the collection, a Tibetan syllable indicating the volume, and the folio number, which is marked as either front (a) or back (b).

1  Gyatso, Tenzin, His Holiness the Dalai Lama, *The Four Noble Truths* (London: Thorsons, 1997), p. 20.

2  *An Anthology* (London: Picador, 1997), p. 382.

3  Cited in Pabongka Rinpoche, *Liberation in the Palm of Your Hand* (Boston: Wisdom Publications, 1991), p. 679.

4  The sixteen aspects, or characteristics, of the four noble truths are: (1) impermanence, (2) suffering, (3) emptiness, and (4) selflessness (the truth of suffering); (5) causes, (6) origin, (7) strong production, and (8) condition (the truth of origin); (9) cessation, (10) pacification, (11) superb, and (12) definite emergence (the truth of the cessation of suffering); (13) path, (14) awareness, (15) achievement, and (16) deliverance (the truth of the path). See Geshe Tashi Tsering, *The Four Noble Truths* (Boston: Wisdom Publications, 2005), p. 148.

5  We find all four seals in the Mahayana Buddhist texts, but in the earlier Pali texts, such as the *Dhammapada*, we find only three marks; the last one (nirvana is true peace) is missing. *Marks* and *seals* have the same connotation.

6 The *lamrim*, or graduated path to enlightenment, is a systematic step-by-step presentation of the teachings of the Buddha that is used in the Gelug tradition.

7 *Abhidharmakosha*, chapter 1; commentary to the root text chapter 1 verse 7 lines A and B. Translation by Geshe Tashi Tsering. For an alternative translation see Leo M. Pruden, *Abhidharmakosabhasyam*, Berkley: Asian Humanities Press, 1988, vol. 1, p. 61.

8 This is dealt with in detail in volume 3 of the *Foundation of Buddhist Thought* series, *Buddhist Psychology*.

9 The thirty-seven aspects of the path to enlightenment are: the four mindfulnesses, the four complete abandonments, the four factors of miraculous powers, the five faculties, the five powers, the seven branches of the path to enlightenment, and the noble eightfold path. See Tenzin Gyatso, the Fourteenth Dalai Lama, *The World of Tibetan Buddhism* (Boston: Wisdom Publications, 1994), p. 20.

10 *Abhidharmakoshabhashyam*, trans. Geshe Tashi Tsering, Derge Tengyur, Abhidharma, vol. *zhu*, f. 43a.

11 Vasubandhu, *Abhidharmakoshabhashyam*, chapter 5; commentary to the root text chapter 5 verse 4. Translation by Geshe Tashi Tsering. For an alternative translation see Leo M Pruden, *Abhidharmakosabhasyam*, Berkley: Asian Humanities Press, 1989, vol. 3, p. 911.

12 Although he did not personally hold Vaibhashika views, it is said that Vasubandhu wrote this text from their point of view. Inevitably there is some debate about this.

13 Purnavardhana, *Abhidharmakosha-lakshanusarini*, trans. Geshe Tashi Tsering, Derge Tengyur, Abhidharma, vol. *zhu*, f. 7b.

14 Chap. 6, v. 4. Translated by Guy Newland in *Appearance and Reality* (Ithaca, N.Y.: Snow Lion Publications, 1999), p. 18.

15 *Abhidharmakoshabhashyam*, trans. Geshe Tashi Tsering, Derge Tengyur, Abhidharma, vol. *chu*, f. 155B.

16 Translated by Georges Dreyfus in *Recognizing Reality* (Albany, N.Y.: State University of New York Press, 1997), p. 69.

17 *Sense organ* does not refer to the gross physical sense organ (the eyeball, nostrils, etc.) but to a very subtle organ that enables the physical organ to apprehend the object's shape, smell, and so on. See Tsering, Geshe Tashi, *Buddhist Psychology*, p. 23.

18 Translated by Guy Newland in *Appearance and Reality*, p. 32.

19 Ibid.

20 Dreyfus, *Recognizing Reality*, p. 67.

21 The Sautrantika concept of selflessness is dealt with in the fifth volume in the *Foundation of Buddhist Thought* series, *Emptiness*.

22 The Chittamatra view of selflessness is dealt with in the fifth volume in the *Foundation of Buddhist Thought* series, *Emptiness*.

23 See Tsering, *The Four Noble Truths*, pp. 116–18.

24 For the Chittamatrins, the realization of coarse selflessness of persons realizes the absence of a permanent, single, independent person, whereas the realization of subtle selflessness of persons realizes the absence of a self-sufficient person. The realization of coarse and subtle selflessness of phenomena (they don't differentiate) realizes that phenomena are not naturally the bases of the names given to them, and that subject and object do not exist as radically distinct and different entities. So all of these can be described as the perfect nature, but in order to attain liberation you only need to realize the coarse and subtle selflessness of persons. See also Hopkins, Jeffrey, *Meditation on Emptiness* (Boston: Wisdom Publications, 1996), p. 299.

25 For an explanation of mind and mental factors, see Geshe Tashi Tsering, *Buddhist Psychology* (Boston: Wisdom Publications, 2006), pp. 21–42.

26 When we finally achieve total cessation, if we do so with this body of contaminated aggregates, the aggregates are still a residue because of their contaminated nature. It is not until the body ceases at death that *nonresidual cessation* occurs. Some bodhisattva practitioners, however, do not enter nonresidual nirvana when they achieve complete cessation but instead stay on to help other beings. For them the next stage is complete enlightenment, and so the stage that would have been nirvana is called *diamond-like samadhi*. According to the Chittamatrins, it is at this point that the mind-basis-of-all ceases.

27 *Vinishchayasamgrahani*, trans. Geshe Tashi Tsering, Derge Tengyur, Chittamatra, vol. *zi*, f. 44a. *Maitreya's Ornament of the Great Vehicle Sutras* (*Mahayanasutralamkara*) also lists five characteristics of ultimate truth, but they are different from those listed here, so for clarity I will stay with Asanga's list.

28 Trans. Geshe Tashi Tsering, Derge Kangyur, Sutrapitaka, vol. *nga*, f. 60b.

29  *Mulamadhyamakakarika*, 24: 8–9, trans. Geshe Tashi Tsering, Derge Tengyur, Madhyamaka, vol. *tsa*, f. 14b.

30  Chap. 9, vv. 1–2. Trans. by Stephen Batchelor in Shantideva, *A Guide to the Bodhisattva's Way of Life* (Dharamsala, India: Library of Tibetan Works and Archives, 1981), p. 131.

31  See, for example, his commentary on Shantideva's Wisdom chapter in *Practicing Wisdom*, trans. by Geshe Thupten Jinpa (Boston: Wisdom Publications, 2005), esp. pp. 16–30.

32  From the commentary to chapter 6 of the *Madhyamakavatara* by Chandrakirti.

33  *Madhyamakavatara*, trans. Geshe Tashi Tsering, Derge Tengyur, Madhyamaka, vol. *a*, f. 205b.

34  *Lankavatara Sutra*, trans. Geshe Tashi Tsering, Derge Kangyur, Sutrapitaka, vol. *ca*, f. 174b.

35  Tsongkhapa, *Ocean of Reasoning: A Great Commentary on Nagarjuna's Mulamadhyamakakarika* (Oxford: Oxford University Press, 2006), pp. 479–80. In the Tibetan text published by the Pleasure of Elegant Sayings Press (Sarnath, India: 1992), this citation can be found on page 402.

36  Sense direct perceivers are our five sense consciousnesses (visual, aural, and so on). Mental direct perceivers are not sense related but also not conceptual, and include the first moment of apprehending an object as well as clairvoyance. Yogic direct perceivers are unmistaken non-sense-related minds generated by higher beings. See Tsering, *Buddhist Psychology*, pp. 130–33.

37  To briefly explain the three modes of a syllogism, take this example from the *Descent into Lanka Sutra*:

The entities of things are like
Appearances [of things] in a mirror,
Which do not exist there
Because of lacking oneness or otherness.

Shantarakshita renders this in syllogistic form:

A) These things propounded by ourselves and others,
B) do not inherently exist, like a reflection,
C) because they lack in reality a nature of unity or plurality.

The *property of the position* means that the sign must be a property of the subject (C must be a property of A). Here, "lacking in reality a nature of unity or plurality" is said to be a property of "things."

The *forward pervasion* means that the sign is pervaded by the predicate (C is pervaded by B). The sign must be a member of the class of phenomena represented by the predicate. This means that "lacking in reality a nature of unity or plurality" is pervaded by "not inherently existing."

The *counter pervasion* means that the negative of the sign is pervaded by the negative of the predicate (−C is pervaded by −B). Thus, anything that did have a nature of unity or plurality would have to exist inherently. (Taken from Dan Haig, *An Analysis of Madhyamika Particle Physics*, www.tibet.org/dan/madhyamaka.)

38  Tsongkhapa Blo bzang grags pa, *Byang chub lam rim che ba.* (Zi ling: Tso Ngon People's Press, 1985), p. 623. Translated here by the author.

39  These distinctions are covered in the fifth book of the *Foundation of Buddhist Thought* series, *Emptiness*.

40  An *arya* is one who has had a yogic direct perception of emptiness. Until one becomes a buddha, this takes place during deep states of meditation. In between states of meditative equipoise, an arya returns to seeing objects as self-existent; however, he or she no longer believes in that appearance.

41  *Prasannapada*, Derge Tengyur, Madhyamaka, vol. *a*, f. 163b. Translation from Tsongkhapa, *Ocean of Reasoning*, p. 487.

42  Tsongkhapa, *Ocean of Reasoning*, p. 487.

43  *Madhyamakavatara*, 6: 23, trans. Geshe Tashi Tsering, Derge Tengyur, Madhyamaka, vol. *a*, f. 208a.

44  In fact, there have been Tibetan teachers historically who have argued just that. The Jonang position, for instance, is that emptiness is in a category all its own and that it is empty merely of everything that is not emptiness, but is itself self-existent. This is the so-called empty-of-other (*zhentong*) position.

45  From the commentary to chapter 6 of the *Madhyamakavatara* by Chandrakirti.

46  *Byang chub lam rim che ba*, p. 626.

47  Again, this is covered in the fifth book of the *Foundation of Buddhist Thought* series, *Emptiness*.

48 *Byang chub lam rim che ba*, trans. Geshe Tashi Tsering, p. 627.

49 *Madhyamakavatara*, 6: 79–80, trans. Geshe Tashi Tsering, Derge Tengyur, Madhyamaka, vol. *a*, f. 208a.

50 A *bhumi* (Sanskrit for "level") is a stage that a bodhisattva passes through to reach enlightenment. There are ten bhumis, and they begin at the first moment of the yogic direct perception of emptiness in meditative equipoise. It is on the eighth bhumi that a practitioner's realization of emptiness becomes immutable.

51 Translated by Thupten Jinpa in *Self, Reality and Reason in Tibetan Philosophy* (Oxford: RoutledgeCurzon, 2002), p. 142. From *Samadhirajasutra*, 9, 11–17. *Samadhirajasutra: Sarva-dharma-svabhava-samatha-vipañcita-samadhi-raja-sutra, Chos tham cad kyi rang bxhin mnyam par spros pa ting nge 'dzin gyi rgyal po'i mdo*, P795, vol. 31.

# INDEX

# About the Authors

GESHE TASHI TSERING escaped Tibet in 1959 with his family at the age of one, and entered Sera Mey Monastic University in South India at thirteen, graduating sixteen years later as a Lharampa Geshe, the highest level. Requested by Lama Thubten Zopa Rinpoche, the spiritual director of the Foundation for the Preservation of the Mahayana Tradition (FPMT), to teach in the West, he became the resident teacher at Jamyang Buddhist Centre in London in 1994, where he developed *The Foundation of Buddhist Thought,* which has become one of the core courses in the FPMT's education program. He has taught the course in England and Europe since 1997.

GORDON MCDOUGALL was director of Cham Tse Ling, the FPMT's Hong Kong center, for two years in the 1980s and worked for Jamyang Buddhist Centre in London from 2000–2006. He has taken an active part in the development and administration of the *The Foundation of Buddhist Thought.*

# FOUNDATION OF BUDDHIST THOUGHT

*The Foundation of Buddhist Thought* is a two-year course in Buddhist studies created by Geshe Tashi Tsering of Jamyang Buddhist Centre in London. The program draws upon the depth of Tibetan Buddhist philosophy to exemplify how Buddhism can make a real difference in the way we live our lives. *The Foundation of Buddhist Thought* is part of the Foundation for the Preservation of the Mahayana Tradition (FPMT) core study program. This course can be taken either in person or by correspondence. It consists of the following six four-month modules:

+ The Four Noble Truths
+ Relative Truth, Ultimate Truth
+ Buddhist Psychology
+ The Awakening Mind
+ Emptiness
+ Tantra

In addition to the related Wisdom book, each module includes approximately fifteen hours of professionally edited audio teachings on either CD, MP3 disc (or download), taken from Geshe Tashi's recent London course. These are used in conjunction with guided meditations to explore each topic in depth. Each student is also part of a study group led by a tutor who facilitates discussions twice a month, helping the student to bring the topics to life through active dialogue with other members of the group. Essays and exams are also an essential part of the curriculum. This mixture of reading, listening, meditating, discussing, and writing ensures that each student will gain an understanding and mastery of these profound and important concepts.

A vital aspect of the course is Geshe Tashi's emphasis on the way these topics affect our everyday lives. Even a philosophical topic such as relative and ultimate truth is studied from the perspective of the choices we make on a daily basis, and the way to begin to develop a more realistic approach to living according to the principles of Buddhist thought.

> "A real life-changer. The jigsaw that was Dharma all suddenly fits into place." —*course graduate*

To find out more about *The Foundation of Buddhist Thought*, please visit our website at **www.buddhistthought.org**. To find out more about FPMT study programs, please visit **www.fpmt.org**.

# About Wisdom

Wisdom Publications, a nonprofit publisher, is dedicated to making available authentic Buddhist works for the benefit of all. We publish translations of the sutras and tantras, commentaries and teachings of past and contemporary Buddhist masters, and original works by the world's leading Buddhist scholars. We publish our titles with the appreciation of Buddhism as a living philosophy and with the special commitment to preserve and transmit important works from all the major Buddhist traditions.

To learn more about Wisdom, or to browse books online, visit our website at wisdompubs.org. You may request a copy of our mail-order catalog online or by writing to:

Wisdom Publications
199 Elm Street
Somerville, Massachusetts 02144 USA
Telephone: (617) 776-7416 ✦ Fax: (617) 776-7841
Email: info@wisdompubs.org
www.wisdompubs.org

## The Wisdom Trust

As a nonprofit publisher, Wisdom is dedicated to the publication of fine Dharma books for the benefit of all sentient beings and dependent upon the kindness and generosity of sponsors in order to do so. If you would like to make a donation to Wisdom, please do so through our Somerville office. If you would like to sponsor the publication of a book, please write or email us at the address above.

Thank you.

Wisdom is a nonprofit, charitable 501(c)(3) organization affiliated with the Foundation for the Preservation of the Mahayana Tradition (FPMT).

# Also available from the
## *Foundation of Buddhist Thought* Series

The Four Noble Truths
Foundation of Buddhist Thought, Volume 1
Geshe Tashi Tsering
192 pages | ISBN 0861712706 | $14.95

In this, the first volume of the *Foundation of Buddhist Thought*, Geshe
Tashi provides a complete presentation the Buddha's seminal Four Noble
Truths, which summarize the fundamentals of the Buddhist worldview.
Indeed, they are an essential framework for understanding all of the other
teachings of the Buddha.

Buddhist Psychology
Foundation of Buddhist Thought, Volume 3
Geshe Tashi Tsering
176 pages | ISBN 0861712722 | $14.95

*Buddhist Psychology* addresses both the nature of the mind and how we
know what we know. Just as scientists observe and catalog the material
world, Buddhists for centuries have been observing and cataloging the
components of our inner experience. The result is a rich and subtle knowledge that can be harnessed to the goal of increasing human well-being.

The Awakening Mind
Foundation of Buddhist Thought, Volume 4
Geshe Tashi Tsering
176 pages | ISBN 0861715101 | $14.95

In *The Awakening Mind*, Geshe Tashi Tsering guides students to a thorough understanding of two of the most important methods for developing
bodhichitta that have been passed down by the great Indian and Tibetan
masters over the centuries: the seven points of cause and effect, and equal-
izing and exchanging the self with others.